Nobody Loves Me

Poems

Abigail George

Mwanaka Media and Publishing Pvt Ltd,
Chitungwiza, Zimbabwe
*
Creativity, Wisdom, and Beauty

Publisher: *Mmap*
Mwanaka Media and Publishing Pvt Ltd
24 Svosve Road, Zengeza 1
Chitungwiza, Zimbabwe

mwanaka@yahoo.com
mwanaka13@gmail.com
https://www.mmapublishing.org
www.africanbookscollective.com/publishers/mwanaka-media-and-publishing
https://facebook.com/MwanakaMediaAndPublishing/

Distributed in and outside N. America by African Books Collective
orders@africanbookscollective.com
www.africanbookscollective.com

ISBN: 978-1-77933-862-4
EAN: 9781779338624

© Abigail George 2024

All rights reserved.
No part of this book may be reproduced or transmitted in any form or by any means, mechanical or electronic, including photocopying and recording, or be stored in any information storage or retrieval system, without written permission from the publisher

DISCLAIMER
All views expressed in this publication are those of the author and do not necessarily reflect the views of *Mmap*.

Table of Contents

Berg
Salinger's wife
Pears, with a knife
River
Auto-immune disease, or, love
Near-anorexia, alcoholism, addiction, self-loathing
The most beautiful thing I can make is this haiku
Healing mother tongue of a hungry poet
Chant of the wild birds in my throat
The ghost fades
It's enough for us to sit in silence and wonder
Stitch me back together again like a tapestry
Energies
I still have proof in the form of scars, wounds, hurting
The sad fact is, beautiful trauma is just like fire, and giving regret the once-over
Like water, like Gillian Slovo
The evolution of Abigail George where there was just an empty space before
Don't waste your pain, it's a symbol of hope in the darkness
Alkaline
When in Rome

The Wisest Ones
Read the books your father read
Leaving My Sorrows Behind
Nazareth
Older
Jeremiah (experimental haiku)
Macroclimate (experimental haiku)
Sappho
Smuts
Napoleon
The Boer Wars
The bear wife
Lull
All roads lead to Grahamstown, come back
Sultanas
She sleeps alone
The Unstable Genius of Jean Rhys

Introduction

The conditioned thinking intellectualism, identity politics and the "silent" evidence of the solitary genius of my father Dr Ambrose Cato George has played a significant role in my development as an essayist and social commentator, as a poetry and cultural practitioner. My father came to Christ, as I did. Religious texts have always held me spellbound. A special book was given to me, the Don't Be Sad book and then I turned to the Quran, I embraced it and wondered to myself how many Christians have done this. What treasure and gems I found there! But did reading the Quran mean I wasn't a Christian anymore? I had so many questions. The flesh hates and punishes others, rejects others, has the approach of stigma against clinical depression but the spirit has will, discipline and stamina on its side. What do you do when the voice of your family is not on your side? It, quite frankly, made me suicidal. All of it. The rejection from the community and the stigma against clinical depression. It made me feel as if I was living a compromised life.

There were three decades of fire during the 1960-1990s in South Africa. Warfare. Psychological warfare. Spiritual warfare. Physical warfare. There's no difference. There's a fallout. There's an aftermath. Picture this. The illusion of reality and I place emphasis on that because what if it becomes a condition where you only begin to see the illusion of reality and nothing else until it becomes a medical model.

In the life of Dr Ambrose Cato George Ph.D, my father, he was recruited into a subversive organization as a student at UWC formerly known as Bush University, he was a scholar who studied at London University, teacher, writer, family man but there was disorder in his life when it came to his mood. A wise and brilliant man, it still occupies his life.

I am sure that many in South Africa identify with my father's life. I am sure that people identify with the importance of the genetic factors in the field of mental health across those decades. I look at his personality, intelligence, politics, recovery and relapse during that tumultuous time of South Africa's history. Perhaps as South Africans we are all quiet revolutionaries.

Men and women had the conviction to risk their lives in exchange for freedom and emancipation. They wanted to liberate the sound mind, body and soul from a terrifying regime. Sought to annihilate and erase oppression, ridicule, mockery, humiliation and systemic racism.

My paternal grandfather was a veteran himself of the Second World War and I am sure there are veterans of the armed struggle who have this narrative in their own story.

I have found when I peruse material concerning the Islamic faith a kind of peace of mind, a silence, a calm acceptance that has no laws governing it pertaining to the status of what car you drive, where you live, the schools your children attend, if you have a university degree. Islam is the fastest growing religion in the world. It has taught me to make a conscientious habit of being kind, tolerant and understanding towards others. It has given me a novel vision for the future, it has given me hope. The old me in that distant life was filled with hardship and despair. Depression, that darkness visible, was the enemy that held me captive in those days.

There is so much going on these days. There is so much to be grateful and thankful for. The church and the poet and cultural practitioner, where do they meet? How do we extract value, access and agency from both? We have to understand and establish the value of what the church, poetry and culture means to the Christian. Since ancient times the Christian has come under fire for blasphemy.

We must ask ourselves what are the intentions of our tribe, your tribe, my tribe, the collective tribe and what are the character traits of your inner circle? We must catch people doing the right thing instead of always playing the name and blame game. I was listening to the Ideas That Matter podcast by Vusi Thembekwayo and found what he talked about refreshing and insightful. It also inspired this missive to the editor.

To reach platforms, for us to express ourselves, elucidate progress and pronounce performance we must build norms, and establish this in our communities, in our homes, in the workplace, and if we are poets and cultural practitioners in our place, in our poetry and cultural environment we must integrate these norms. As Christians we must build these same norms in church and our interpersonal relationships.

We must, as Vusi Thembekwayo said in his podcast, "catch people doing the right thing".

Berg
(twelve-haiku for the poet Arthur Nortje)

Despair it hurts much –
To love not just to possess.
You're monk. I'm poet.

You are watching me –
They will ultimately let-you-down-badly.
Don't be so jealous.

Of the divine fetching-couples –
People, you give them chances (let them go).
I am older. No-longer-foolish-girl.

Sleep has her mansion –
Plastic flowers literally-on-the-graveside.
I'm afraid of life.

After a-harsh winter –
Reality was like jazz-climate.
Not just a shipwreck.

Anna Kavan is rain, leaf –
Becoming a writer like-Flannery-O'Conner.
The berg is Hamlet.

Stars let me alone.
Everything was so quiet.
Sign the bee treatise.

Writing must change you –
In-the-albino haired prison of my head.
Triumph was unknown.

Rooms filled with antiques –
This house belongs to kismet.
Furniture bought on impulse.

Rosa Parks was right –
Pray for me. Pray for my fragmented-soul.
The pain in my life.

Call me by my name –
Muscular-beefy boy trending. Prize and star.
I want a tall guy-as-tall-as-rooftops.

I am yours, Lazarus –
Plant me near a stream-of-water in bone-season.
Set me free guardian.

Salinger's wife
(twelve-haiku for Neville Alexander's mother)

Abandoned cottage –
Salinger is standing man.
Wife came with the tide.

She dreamed of waltzing –
The ice was dead to her. Numbed-her-to-her-soul.
Her life was lonely.

Spells an offering –
Miserable rain don't call-or-touch-her.
The image of death.

She studied snowflakes –
Fear, fears are what she held dear.
Her goals, animals.

Pale king exquisite –
Worm country under a magnifying-glass.
Now wild voyager.

Lamb to the slaughter –
The mad life of writers-who-are poets.
She's in a tunnel (making her escape).

Walking alone in this world –
Text sparkles in silence, in-the-hours.
You sapped-up his knowledge.

Snow. Sleeping too much –
The unplanned days makes for pearls.
Tabloid-stares wasted on me.

I killed the tattoo –
I drowned it in the cold purple-sea.
Kept watch over rabbit.

The wedding was nice –
And fossils found underground.
She hung lace curtains.

The pastor must come –
Salinger is writing at-full-speed-ahead.
The children must come.

The honeymoon phase –
African violets bloom in-the-garden.
Worlds-in-them full of stories.

Pears, with a knife
(twelve-haiku for the poet Dennis Brutus)

The muse is a poet –
Anticipation marked me.
Peaches voice of Eve.

Crazy glory boys –
That summer we headed west.
Kissing the velvet.

Alaska is too-cold –
The destinations random.
You have been loved.

Wisconsin fever –
Letting go of emptiness.
Tears. All is not well.

That day on the beach –
Eating toast in solitude.
Searching for fig roots.

Lovers of poets –
Predestined-woman in the old photograph.
Sex in the afternoon.

Now this makes me sad –
I'm loving you in secret.
Strange day. Winter rain.

Wild birds gathering –
When a stranger shows up holding-on.
Crestfallen blue hills.

Swimming in rivers –
Sad church on Sunday mornings.
We're wolves. The hunters.

It could just be talk –
My sister doesn't like you.
To do this to wise-me.

Let's get physical -
Think of loving lovers putting-them-far-away.
I say the wrong things.

Social paradigms –
Solitary-figure. Fundamentals of life.
We're aloes in bloom.

River
(a series of thirteen haiku for my mother)

Devilish Swiss clock –
Hours go by. Took a nap (in a swimming pool).
Drowning. Curse or gift.

You're in my bloodline –
Jurisdiction. Rainbow child (raped, raped, raped).
Matters of the heart.

Sea girl. Sea boy. Animals –
I've got flowers in the spring. (Garden City Clinic).
Birds find their way-so-will-I.

Little mouse. You're loved –
You're a charming little mouse (short story lover).
Blood axe to the heart.

Solo. Soul and life –
Psychology of gang-hate (shoot to kill, kill, kill).
Disturbing nature.

Water. Sleep. Music –
No family. Just this tattoo (made with a razor blade).
Prayer and church life.

Introducing inter-faith –
Grief wounds. Psychology in-words-and-scenarios.
Somehow it anchors.

You're a fake river –
This tanned-brown skin does not exist.
She stood there crying.

None of her friends came –
The funeral was a sad-affair.
Now I'm a poet.

Wiser than the beach –
No more cooking for her. No kitchen-tables.
No more warm beers.

I go to the lake –
Remember the posh clinic.
Got to call collect.

This body is ghost –
I'm a dangerous woman (to be around with).
Away drift the years.

Eat sea creatures –
Insomnia is wretched (you're gone, you're gone).
The wine sates me.

Auto-immune disease, or, love
(a series of thirteen-haiku for my sister)

You're my potential –
A husband will change your life.
Make you gentler. Kind.

Cage the sunlight –
All the years we never spoke.
That's karma for you.

Rivers of bloodlines –
Never had a phantom-wife or those
Aspects of lovers.

She stood there laughing –
Hands on her hips, never to-breathe-again
In-my-life as wise as blood.

I'll never learn Czech –
The way that she'll learn it.
Birds are made of bones.

Swimming pool. Ghost limbs –
Everywhere you look, birds-birds-wild-birds.
This love poem for Prague.

See you Christmas then –
We'll Skype, send-emails. Video call.
See you next birthday.

Blood axe to the heart –
Thread forgiveness into the-hems-of-your-garments.
Class never to live-again.

Wild heart just like fire –
Vintage clothing, furs, snow. Things.
Whatever you want.

Flatlet with kitchen –
Vases made in China by-a-female-factory-worker.
Boyfriend and lover.

Your Prague. It's yours. Yours –
I won't be in any of-your-photographs.
I won't see any-of-its scenes.

You never phoned. Wrote –
You're in God's surreal strong hands.
Cape Town was yours. Yours.

Past tense. Blood sisters –
You never loved me back. Nothing-to-say.
Cat got your tongue. Spill.

Near-anorexia, alcoholism, addiction, self-loathing
(for Dorothy West)

Nirvana is dead –
Mythic, sparse, and like music.
Golden inner child.

Down the school hallways –
Pack your glory-days away for good.
Survival kit for-karma.

Put your sass away.
And so, we master trauma (for mankind).
High school is over.

Stop pushing yourself –
After the winter's exchange.
Call the bee police.

Master of walking –
You promised me a sprung ark.
Remember Berlin.

I'm youngish woman –
Take the pills to numb the pain.
Call the therapist.

The art of undone –
Grief champion. Daughter, speak.
In this bone season.

Greece is key master –
The wonder boys of the Corps.
Cold sun, look at me.

We enter our wounds –
Sing gospel like priestesses.
Marry cute prophets.

A plate of doubt. Eat -
Coward, bliss drunk on language.
A glass of wine. Drink.

Consume without awe –
Radical thinker eating-prickly-pears, plums.
The passion of sand.

Make, heal disaster –
Plant my body near the sea.
Lipstick memories.

The stars are nosy –
River running through it close-to-bone.
Believe in fossils.

The most beautiful thing I can make is this haiku
(for my mother, sister, brother, and father)

Air. Heir can't be cured –
I'm bee farmer caught stealing.
Hospitality.

Swallows flit in the air –
Only the houndish-rain can cure me.
The don't know regret.

The nature of green –
They don't know the dishes are-waiting.
You keep telling me.

Hours pass in nothings –
Or home. Or harm. Only song.
The other side telling.

I said that just now –
My sister cut her hair. Narrative-repeated.
Looking through a lens.

I can't leave the house –
Because I'm afraid that people are laughing (at me).
Branches reach for me.

I dream of healing –
But it's just a mapped out tap-root.
I saw a wo/man.

Called tongue slippage –
Blue night is coming for me.
Yonder it is dark.

Hoping for applause –
Wild seabirds don't hope for that.
For sonnets, marriage.

My room with a view –
It's also my prison with-a-view.
Woolf can't be trusted.

Left me for wide-eyed dead –
My love killed me with one shot.
Raised his rifle wide.

Swum like an otter –
Needed the energy in-my-body.
The stars were needles.

My blood was in tubes –
To test thyroid functioning.
Nurse, leave me alone.

Healing mother tongue of a hungry poet
(for my mother, sister, brother, and father)

(Wild) visible flowers –
It's Gustav Mahler in June.
June is my birthday.

Signs of sunflowers –
Joop is a perfectionist.
I'm just obsessive.

Woolf to the lighthouse –
I don't want to be unseen (anymore).
It is bone season.

With love, and squalor –
I am going mad again.
Shadows of your wings.

Mourning wind and rain –
The non-supportive members of the family.
Hate is a strong word.

My flesh longs for you –
Think of Moses in the wild.
The soul of a wo/man.

Red plum of a spoilt baby –
I think of you, and go mad.
Flush in each cheek bone.

So, I take the anti-depressants –
They call me 'mental', 'black sheep'.
Somehow, that calms me.

This seed, mad life roots –
They go deep, ninja warrior.
Gone-forever to the races.

Despair and hardship –
Photographs make me forget (the haters, the lovers)
The non-reality of pastor.

I long for the wild-and-wilderness –
I read-research-write pamphlets on wellness.
I repeat myself (odd).

This pull-and-push towards health –
Info on the hush of the-art-world (elephants stomping in the room).
Circles in the Knysna-woods.

Chant of the wild birds in my throat
(for my mother, sister, brother and father)

   My mother never taught me things
(mostly nothings). My mother never told
me that she loved me. My mother
never spoke to me again after she
dumped me at Tara. That godforsaken
posh mental institution in the middle
of Sandton city in the asphalt jungle
of Johannesburg. Will you ever forgive
me? Will you, will you tell me that
you love me? Hold me east and west
back. Hold me back now with your
slow hands of fire, before I finally let

   you go to Prague where you'll learn Czech.
Before I surrender you to international
China, before you interview Paris.
You saved my life again and again and
again. Do you love me, kind sir, knight
with your shining horse? I am so pale.
Nobody has ever told me that they loved
me. Nobody has ever held me so close,
and made me promise not to waste
my life, answered the phone when it's
my number. Roxette said it must have
been love but it is over now. It's where
the river flows, it's where the river flows,

   it's where the wind blows. She glows,

she glows like the wick of a candle.
I glow the candle out. It is done. It is
done. Now I have to get on with the
idea of living with you, and living without
you. I choose you, and reconciliation.
For you are promised to me, and I just
want to praise you, take you at your
word. Out stain, out stain. Spot of wine, of
blood. You don't love me anymore.
Dear, doubt, fear, anxiety, shame. Shame.
Breakthrough, love, or break through,
this is the meaning of breakthrough,

    my love. Will you ever forgive me for
everything, everything that I said, that
I did. Chameleon. Young complicated
boy, confident swagger now. Tall, dark,
and handsome. Look at me, he says. Of
course, I forgive you he says. I've loved
you from afar all my life, want nothing
but the best for you, I worship and
adore you. Want to for the rest of my life.
Obey, honour, submit. They were just
words before. Your pour great fire and
life into the words obey, honour and submit.
I am yours; I am yours, yours, yours.

The ghost fades
(for my mother, sister, brother and father)

I miss you. I don't miss you. I miss you. I really
don't care if you care, I don't miss you. Your
head is Muir and full of devil-may-care girls, with
fluff for hair, and who smell like you're shielding
them from war, and the Cape Corps, and you don't
need me like I need you, and you don't love me
like I love you, and I'm so full of it, so full of myself, of the knowledge
of superego, and manic-depression, and I hear
and see hallucinations. There I said it. There I

said it, and there's another reason for you to hate
me, to never love me, to never leave her for me.
All I can think of is my grandfather, and all I can
think of is his bicycle, and his brother who committed
suicide, and his wife, and all his children who I
love, who I hate, who are estranged from me, and
the cousins who hate to love me, who love to
hate me, who I worship in return. Come back, Oupa, Ouma,
George Botha, Moses Molelekwa, Kevin Carter,

but you're dead to me, but not to another woman,
and I'm having difficulty in guarding my tongue, I
have difficulty in controlling what I think, and what
I say. And the whole earth is filled with your glory,
my paternal grandfather, and you're set adrift, and
I won't rest until your story is told on your terms.

And my love, what does it matter that I can't have
the man that matters to me the most in the world, that
he matters to just about every other single female.

I love you; I love you; I love you, but you don't
love me, adore me, or worship, or praise me but
these words are enough. These words are enough,
and today I thought about the hallucinations, and
the flowers and the fact that you did not want to help me,
instead you hurt me, but it was on my terms, and
these words are on my downtrodden region, and
my terms are my terms. Love, love, love, my love.
If you can't be mine be hers, be hers my love, be hers.

It's enough for us to sit in silence and wonder
(for my great-uncles Lenny and Dennis)

Love is an echo from my distant past, it has bewitched the deep of my soul. I'm living in a cage. It is swell, and ancient, and beautiful there, except that I'm longing to see my love. Your name is horizontal, your love is like a disease, and all I want is pleasure. This is the end of tenderness and inspiration, this is the end of lust and silence is translated into the accompaniment of joy, and these books are singing to me joyfully. In the bedroom it is night and day, and I think of Joe Biden. How strong

and handsome he is, how he buried a son. How I did not bury my dead great-uncle who hung himself from the rafters in an outside toilet. This is what the world is coming to. There's tenderness in the break of day, the breaking of the waves, the sure vibrations in them, the vigour of the sun. And all I can think of is death, and death by suicide, and how there are no photographs of my paternal grandfather's siblings. Dennis was a ruffian... and died a ruffian's death. The daughters were blonde,

and now they are dead too. The root of the flame is found in space, and environment, and cause, and the issue of blood. I know everything there is to know about the issue of blood. I carry endometriosis inside of me, in much the same way I carry infertility. Lenny come back. Dennis come back. Winifred and Bea, let down your ringlets. I want to go to Jamestown. I want to go to Saint Helena. I want to find myself there amongst Napoleon's flora, and fauna. And for the first time in my life I feel that I matter.

Company does not anchor me; it is strangers that anchor me. I am fading, fading, fading away. How strange to see this kind of decay in someone as young as me. 40-years young. This is the end of me, the end of me writing like this, writing poetry like this. And the more I think of my great-uncle's suicide, the more I think about death. He's a chameleon, he's an aroma, he's a man with some incident of childhood trauma in his life. And I am a woman with some incident of childhood trauma in my own blind life.

Stitch me back together again like a tapestry
(for my mother, father, sister, and brother)

I think of your arrival. I think of the love
I feel for you. I think of your departure. I
think of the love I feel for you. When I'm
the planet, you're the universe, stars colliding

in galaxies to the consternation of the other
galaxies. This is a love poem. This is a love
poem. You're the climate, but I'm the weather
forecast. You're trending, while I make a

video call, or text you. You have breath, and
the bloodline of a phoenix. A phoenix turning
in the pure air, tender, and an innocent in
my arms. My love will always keep you as safe
as houses, as safe as sonnets, and you will

come to no harm, my love. I sit here, thinking.
Thinking of you mostly, and often. Of you
swimming, or golden memories. They're a
kind of holy smoke now. They remind me of
the sweetness of life. A woman in love is a

romantic. You make me smile, laugh, walk,
dance, write away the hours, on the inhale. On
the exhale I'm afraid that love has made me even
more fragile. Your mouth tastes like the sea.
The birth of something else written on body.

Energies
(for Petya Dubarova and Iris Shun-Ru Chang))

There's a song inside my head
that I can't get rid of, and I'm
so tired of angry words, and the
darkness in my life. I'm insecure,
and vulnerable, afraid of being
alone, sleeping alone, sleeping
with you, and without you, and
intimacy just like my mother was,
afraid of marriage, whatever is
expected of me, afraid of the infatuation-
phase, the honeymoon-phase,
being married for years, or just a
while. Fear, and anxiety are the motivating
factor for just about everything
in my life. Forget, forgive every whisper
over the trees in the forest. The
shroud, the veil of rain that covers
the trees. Thinking about you, and
all the things you said. Your voice,
you turn me on a lonely night. You
make me forget about struggle,
and major depression while I wash
the dishes, sip green tea, thinking
about the past blooming, posing, laughing
like children, your arms around my waist,
blooming like Khalil Gibran, Rumi,
faded chrysanthemums, and prayer

as holy, and monstrous as chandeliers.
I'm still the perfect daughter, the
forlorn, and sad depressive-socialite.
There's the language of blood, and
scars for the poet Petya Dubarova
in me tears. I weep for her nation,
her heritage, her lyricism, her words.
She was wounded, I am wounded.
Phoenix, she hurt, and I am hurting.
You're a dangerous man, and I'm a
dangerous woman. I'm looking for
answers, calling my mother, she's
captain, on this beautiful morning
looking for sanity, for forgiveness,
so broken-hearted, this sober ache.
There's a bowl of barley soup on
the table. It is most delicious, yum,
but it doesn't pass my lips. I adore
you, but he chose not to live with me,
and I will sometimes imagine that
my spirit is walking alongside his.
There should be an award for these
wild birds, the arrangement of his
hand in mine, the accompaniment of
the symphony of his kiss, the honest
way I want to touch his sea-face.
He doesn't see Africa in the mirror
in the way that I do. Only the past.

I still have proof in the form of scars, wounds, hurting
(for Charlotte Perkins Gilman)

God's will is always healing,
always purposefully-crafted,
and as theology it stands on
its own. In my hands, you're
a mountain, you are handsome,
you are perfect. You eat my pasta,
and say it's delicious. Forget
about the past, you wild-thing
said. How could I leave you on
a wild and autumn-eyed weekend.
Watch me fade away, call you
cometh, and ark, you kiss the
waterfall of her hair, left me far
behind. I come out of the water
after paying my future tithes.
When I was a child my parents
watched pornographic material
in front of us. The breakthrough
came yesterday. The love is telling
me to leave the only home I've ever
known. Spies are coming out of
the driftwood. I don't feel good
anymore, and people ignore me,
and my cries for help. Slow hands.
Take these dysfunctional hands.
Nobody loves me anyway. She

might as well be as good as dead.
She is ghost. Vincent is fasting yogi,
Rooka does not love me anymore.
I am not Ophelia going mad,
noose around my neck, I'm mouse,
am horse. I'm young, I'm German,
sleeping like the dead in a grave.
For a while I lived like the Russians,
the poets, the composers, the writers.
I lived like Tchaikovsky, Antigone,
Nietzsche, Rilke, Susan Sontag.

The sad fact is, beautiful trauma is just like fire, and giving regret the once-over
(for the poet Sara Teasdale)

Tonight, my heart is open, and yet
I'm feeling rough, this tough-bird,
I'll forget you now when I open the
liquid-brown of my eyes, you are the
only man I can express my heart's
 war, my loneliness to. You're mine, love, but
you belong to another, and as a man
you belong to the world. Your smile
is angelic, and I know you feel it too.
The unbearable loneliness in the
 early hours of the morning, as the night breaks into
day, divine intuition, the passage of
waiting for intimacy on the exhale, calling
the love song between the lit flame, I
am here, but you're not. You took your
love, took another, had a child, forgot
me, and now I'm waiting here for love.
I'm voyeur, waiting for you, studying you,
loving you, while you love another.
 And the moonlight, the stars sing
your glory, your hair feels like soft
 rain Mishka, and your shadow is sore, in a dress
looking like regret. I'm in love with
my cousin, I'm in love with my brother-
in-law, a man who once was my film
lecturer, a man who taught me English

in high school but they've all gone away now,
and all I'm left with is the spell they put
me under, Hemingway's short stories,
female poets who collapsed and fell apart,
and because of the chemistry of their
brain took their own life. Think of me,
or don't think of me with my German-
ancestry, sunbathing my pale-king-skin,
think of my sobriety, fake tan, and nobody loves
me, and that's the truth. You certainly don't
anymore. Mishka has Stuart. Stuart has
Mishka, and I, I have no one. No love.
I think of the street lights, when the
sun comes up. I watch the dark skies
turn into blue, the branches as-black-
as-shade, the night turns into a breakthrough.
The men in my life leave, leave, leave.
The males in my life have given me
paradise, worlds, opera and classical
music, words and they taught me to be
myself, on my own. They call me love,
I call them love, or loves, or lovers, or
ex. Fire leaves at the end of the day, and
so does the flame of regret, snow, the
man, in my life, the woman in my life, if
my mother had just loved me just a little, said she was proud
of me, instead of calling me "mistake".

Like water, like Gillian Slovo
(for my slave ancestry)

    We walk in darkness, in circles,
buried in our sins. I don't want to
crush your heart, your flaming lips,
with the concept of grief and the
narrative of the closure of flesh, with
an arrow-like mentorship. You left
me long ago, years in fact, mentored
me to death, and I dreamed of Hemingway's
Paris, brief lives glittering with so
much truth, storytelling, mental anguish,
health short stories doing the bipolar-
dance with Zelda Fitzgerald, drinking
in champagne, pleasure is a disease. You
taught me that I am the bone-thin
woman with peacock-blue eyeshadow on
the lids of my eyes, singing about "educated
fleas" doing it, and it is cold outside
and all I want to do is cry in your arms.
Stinking, saturated winter, innocent,
compelling, enthralling leaf outside
my window, this holy prayer, fast, and
meditation, vision of the indigenous-
Khoi in the primitive Kalahari of Africa.
You don't call me, you don't write to me
send emails, text or Skype. You're like
a ghost nation on lithium, Some things
change about his face when he is with his
son. He promised me a lifetime, and I

stand and watch (working on my second
novella that he'll never find the time to read)
him from afar, with the perspective
of a child, Khoi-moon, Khoi-sun, Khoi-
planets in alignment with the entire
universe, and I think to myself just
how much I love this man, and just
how much he's hurt me, promised to
return to me, but never did, and chief
I'll wake up high sometimes, living
to love you, adore you, praise and worship
all the stars for you, be by your side,
maturing in confidence as a writer, poet,
nothing else. But when you're home
the Playboy bunnies are gold in moonlight.
All Amy Winehouse cared about in the
end was hope, and triumph, and nirvana.
All Kurt Cobain cared about was wanting
to be held tight, to have his wife by his
side. It was what I would have wanted in
those final hours. I am living by myself
in this mansion-hotel. In this beautiful
house I eat soup. The sea belongs to the
pilgrims, Columbus, the Portuguese, the
colonials, the Dutch East India Company, and
there are young women searching for
love, but I'm not one of them. And there
are young men searching for love, but
I'm not interested in the madness fear
of being alone, and having children not
to be alone, to look after me when I'm

old, loneliness and silence does not protest, only witness. Love of my life, there's nothing like the smell of rain after a night of making love, the shape of winter, or your beloved in your arms. You're an angel made of bone, and auditory hallucination, and you make me live; you are worthy of it all.

The evolution of Abigail George where there was just an empty space before
(for my slave ancestry)

    To look at me you wouldn't say that
I was on the brink of death once, suicide,
a succession of deaths, a season of difficulty,
and I take such pleasure from the comfort
of strangers, and the abuse, the pain, the break
when it came was negative, bitter, but that
was my assignment, and woebegone in the
face of an ex-lover, in the face of lust, and
perversion I let go of you for my own sanity,
and now peace makes sense to me, and I want
to impact the world, find purpose in my pain.
I need to heal, take these defeated-wounds,
these everlasting-scars it is law. The testimony
is to forgive the person who has betrayed
me the most. I can help other people who
has fallen, that is my gift. I think of old age
in poverty, instrumental like a symphony calling,
I wanted to hide away in the desert, decay
instead of bloom in the wilderness, and sometimes,
the pain was a sign, the breakthrough was
for a purpose, a missionary-phase is coming
reminding me of the ancient past. I miss you.
I miss our conversations genius-savant. I hope
you're happy with that girl with the brown eyes.
I hope you're really making her happy, I hope
she's making you happy bachelor-man. There
are happy hearts making happy hearts. I inherited

sadness from my mother, everything was everlasting
in my childhood, doubting always doubting
confession, and the light in his eyes, but I'm off
the coast, not relying on people of the aloes,
of the street lights, of Bethelsdorp, and Bethesda,
Schauderville, and Sidwell, and there are sad
women, and lonely men who are broken inside,
waiting for their pieces to deal their currency, compliment
the climate change of their intelligence. You can't

change your destiny, shake off the disrespect,
the hurting, and the clothes that I'm wearing say
I'm a painter like Van Gogh, philosopher like Freud,
and I'm a lazy-writer that has seeds of applause,
and greatness on the inside of me. If only you
had liked me, loved me through the depression.
I'm singing your song again, tall in your world,
principled, courageous, valued, and confident.
Highly-favoured, and motivated, and I was looking
to you to save me, but you didn't, or couldn't
put out the bowl of fire out in my eyes. I still
love you like yesterday when all my troubles seemed
so far away, and I've lived a limited education.
I inherited the rain, and an astrologer from my mother,
and there was an offering of boating for beginners.

Don't waste your pain, it's a symbol of hope in the darkness
(for my slave ancestry)

Shroud don't say anything if I changed
my hair, if I spoke my thoughts, don't
move an inch, a muscle. There's a knot
in your throat. It is just a moment in the
falling light. Kissing the velvet of your
shoulder. Stay, stay with me, hold me if
you dare. Truth matters to me. Leave me
another day. Love me another day. I know
you still need to heal. The temptation
to kiss you, to hold you is so strong, love.
I think of the unbearable loneliness into
the early hours of the morning. Stay with
me, dark is the night, the shapes crying
in the rain that go together. At the end of
the day I am tired, the love is gone, the
love is there. Everyone that I love, leaves
me, and in return I leave them in the heat
and the dust, the rust moth, India, the ex-
waves lapping at the shore. You're my life-
line, and I'll be forever writing love poems
to reach you. If only R. could look at me
that way again, instead of as if I came from
   another planet from outer space. Men,
the older male in particular expects sex, and
women expect nothing but love in return. Sins
are found in winter like books, the curator
of a museum writing his report. Nobody
calls Petrovna on the telephone. Asks her

out on dates. Her ex is in love, a perfect
love, and she gives him tenderness, and a
romantic love, her lips softly chant sweet
nothings when they make love, her physical
body is just as enchanting, his high euphoric.
All in love, but nobody loves me, all I keep
finding is wild onions forever not yours.
You are an angel R. You look angelic like a
groom, still as handsome as life, as breath,
as a wild Saturday. He sings, he trusts, he speaks
French while I shy away for an autumn,
while I'm forever not his, forever not yours.

   And I'm battling to survive between
anxiety, and fear of the unknown, the elite
white bikini-pressures of summer, talking
away. R.'s aura is a palace filled with longing,
and belonging, graceful silence. Beneath it
all I'm sad, underneath it all I feel shame.
And the field is divided between what R. shall
sew, and what he will reap. The music is so
sad that it touches my soul. I'm battling mountains,
hiking, climbing through the greenness of
valleys. R.'s lover is velvet, like a Wednesday evening
sweeter than any wine, swimming for survival
   and I'm slipping away tonight. Dawn breaks,
like touch, like a river, like the sleeping sea.

Alkaline
(for my paternal grandparents)

I'm alone. I'm alone again, a solitary figure thinking
ever after of you, for you are the love of Ophelia's life,
of you, and the ownership of daughters in a maze, the
race question, the class system when in Rome. You
either love me, or you don't. You either care for me
or you don't. Once my flesh was a prize, now I'm older,
wiser, but what to do with this knowledge, there's no
exit out of this soldiering on, sleeping alone, waking
alone, and I'm surrounded by star-people who work
miracles on me. I trust so hard, I let the sun go down
on me, summers are cold, winters are cold, they whisper
of their neuroses to me, and I'm asking for forgiveness,
and I'm asking to be loved, and I'm asking you to fall
in love with me if you dare, she's transformed into

matter, particles, atoms, molecules, air, Norma Jean
and Marilyn, and I can't accept anything that is less than
love, or reading the wonderland-feeling of your body, and
I think of your gravity, meeting my gravity, your air
meeting my outspoken lips, my hair, my shoulders, and
I want to bring you down, give you all the love that I
can give, instead I'm sleeping alone, and you're with her,
you're with the love of your life, and I only fell asleep
in the early hours of the morning, the night was hell to
tell you the truth, because you weren't here if you want
to know. I've been listening to Coldplay the entire
morning, trying not to think of you kissing the love of
your life, while I'm here on my own. You think you

know me, you think you've fallen in love, but I'm ghost.

I'm fattened ghost, self-conscious ghost, it feels like it did when I was little. I miss you waking up in the morning. I'm not intimidated by your lady friends anymore, just scared-competent. You can love whomever you want, show me mercy, show me grace, make me cry because you're so good at doing that to me anyway, and this funny woman loves you so much, would do anything for you. And then I woke up as if from a grassroots-dream, glee, fragile, how to live without you, this fire catching fire, and I think of the journey and direction of the misunderstood flame, and everything is psychological guesswork, my jealousy is magnificent, my love is abundant and needs permission from you to exist, all I have is this organic depression, this pilgrimage. Delete all of that.

When in Rome
(for my paternal grandparents)

You and that see-through dark-haired girl, you love
her, don't you. Let me count all the ways you love her.
I could be dead, or just missing, or just missing out
on you. Your name is a song inside my head, and mob
justice burns bright tonight. There's so much of you
in the narrative and context of my stories. There will
always be so much of you. And we were never lovers,
nor boyfriend and girlfriend, just a crack in the system,
and you know how much I love you, and you know
about my nervous breakdown, that I never finished
high school, and I know you want to be a family-man,
I know you want to build a home; I know you want
to belong, but life means different things to us, to us.
My home is the world, my home is under Scandinavian
skies, my home is sexy-Swaziland, minor earth and

major sky. Your lips are like velvet, and my face is
made of stone. I think you're the epitome of cool, want to
kiss you so much, pull you in real close, but you're in
love with a dark-haired girl now, and I have to respect
you, and remember you, and remind you I loved you too,
I loved you before she did, I loved you first. It's
lonely out here blogging away in this frozen wilderness,
but writing brings an order to my life, and my neck is
graceful, and you'll never see me naked, it has been too
long, and so many things have gone unsaid between us.
So, this is goodbye then my loyal friend until I see you
in heaven. And I'm going to cry Argentina, there's nothing

you can do about that. We could have been lovers. We could have been lovers. We could have been lovers. And I'm not maternal, although my throat has a masculine energy.

The Wisest Ones
(for mummy and daddy, who believed)

You're the star signs of a fortunate man
in realms. I won't fly into you again. You
won't come around like clockwork on a
Sunday evening. I think I love you. You
never say the same. So, I guess that's my
answer then. Wish me luck. Wish you luck.
I'm a flame. I'm a flame in a pantomime.
Look out for the sleeping satellite. Souls
are like the rooms in a mansion. You're

gone into the arms of another woman.
You're velvet, but taste like regret. Guess
this is goodbye. Or just a veil. I've romanced
you. You've seduced me. I'm learning that
I'm a celestial. You're free. I thought we'd
be together forever. You're nearly a married
man, my friend. Could have been me. But
would we have been happy? I could never
have given you the children you wanted.

I know you would have been satisfied with
one. Sleeping with her, your muse, she's fallen.
Goodbye mysterious lover. Goodbye never
boyfriend. Goodbye for never given you a
real chance at loving me. Again, I'm dying
inside. Whatever this is, I look within. I say

goodbye with my head held high. Guess I
won't be invited to the wedding, or, the wedding
reception. Too much history there. Here. In the dark.
Goodbye, old friend. To your new life. We

won't be sharing anything together anymore.
I thought you always were half-ashamed of me.
Didn't know we could have spent eternity
together. So much wasted potential, so much
pain. I'll always understand you. You me. I
wish you and your future wife all the gladness
and happiness in the world. It won't be with
me. So much wasted time. I let the years go
by. You were loved. Take that with you. You

were cherished friend once. Now you're in
love. Don't return my phone calls. You're
free. I understand everything now. Look at me.
My smile stays on while my heart is breaking.
Nobody wants to love wretched me. Let go.
I'm already gone. Faded into memory. Don't
speak. Don't speak. You do that so well, so well.
I will always love you. That is all I am taking with
me. Tears and joy. And the despair of loneliness.

We want the same thing. Just not with each other.
We desire other people to fill those hours.
You don't love me in the way I need to be
loved. You see, I want a man who deserves me.
You want a woman who deserves you. Who fits your
high profile. I'm not the one. I'm not the one.

If I was, you'd be here now, not in hiding.
She'll be your wife. She'll be your wife, and it
cuts like a knife. I had feelings for you once, once.

I've surrendered you to the universe. It gave
you a wife. You never came around all that
often anyway. You're feeling good. I'm feeling the
blues. Your wife is your hope now. Your hands.
I'm no superwoman. Don't even have a
man to call my own. No one to love. Those
days are long gone. No one. No one like the
one I love. I've gone the distance. Followed
my heart. Tell you something. Must be karma.

Read the books your father read
(for mummy and daddy, who believed)

I waste time. I waste time. When I do, I cry.
I don't need a shield for that. To display
emotion. I'm more together now than I've
ever been. I'm letting go. I'm saying goodbye.
You're still beautiful to me. This morning
the love of my life said that she didn't care
for me, to listen to me. Perhaps sisters are
like that. I don't love the men anymore. They've
gone to the cemetery of the mind. I'm not

ashamed of anything I've done. I don't have
any regrets. I never started a war. Conflict
makes my blood boil. Once I was under his spell,
but he never chose me. Did not love me. He
wanted to hide me away from the world.
Your sad songs stopped my heart. They kill
me now. I tried to fall in love, I failed, but I'm
wiser now. I tried to teach him that I was hurt
too, but he walked right on by, said goodbye.

I wanted to say, please don't go, but he didn't
give me a chance. He just made me wise. Don't
dedicate anything to me, he said. I'm not that
kind of person. Did Einstein have fangs like me,
did he love like me? For sure science stopped his
heart like it does me. You were always there. I am
in space dementia, my collective soul feeling

megalomaniac. I've been bruised black and blue. I've been wounded, eyes on fire with no cash.

Time has all the answers, whether you want to decode the moon, the planets, the sun, or just want to love, fall in love, leave a lover. My lungs are made of iron, and flightless bird. I want it all. I want everything. Who will I love eventually? Who will love me for a lifetime, an eternity? I'm tired of waiting. It feels like I've been waiting forever. There are micro cuts on my fake heart. Say that you will love me anyway. He's gone.

Leaving My Sorrows Behind
(for mummy and daddy, who believed)

And all I want to be is where the boys are, the
guys. The older men with their ways, premium
brand of cigarettes. Take me up there all the time.
Take me. Take me to the museum. Take me to
the muscle museum. Teach me to love him. Teach
me to care for him. To bury my secrets deep.
Encore. Nothing like love to heal the broken-
hearted. Encore, after encore. I'm falling like a flightless bird. A
flightless little bird, scared-shitless, yet still flying.

And I still believe in freedom, you know that.
You're king. Your land is king. Your ocean-sea is
king. Together we go. I'm going to make a mistake.
I'm going to get gone. No one loves me in this
place. Waiting for someone to save me is a useless
exercise. It kills me to say this that nobody loves
me like I do. That I matter like nuclear energy to
no one. I'm fucking priceless. Love me for me. No
one's around. So, I walk alone. Always on my own.

No more hurt now. Only triumph. No more trials.
Step back wolf. Don't embrace me. I'm a ghost
in the wilderness. Ghosts don't change no one. Just
an illusion shaped like a human being though. Your
love sure looks good to me. I've seen better days.
River of dark nights upon me again. Save me, why
don't you save me my love, love, and old friend;

you're all loved up now with kids on the way. I need you, but nobody needs me. I'm dead to the world.

It came from Japan. It came from Hiroshima's lonely. You cut her. He cut her. You cut her hair. She sleeps alone. This rain that is falling is a miracle. No one wants that person's reflection in the mirror. No one wants to love her, to love me. Nobody misses her. Even her words are lonely. She remembers all of their wounds, her wounds, his wounds. She's torn the miracle now. Turned paradise into hell. But she's an athlete. So, endures.

Nazareth
(for my sister, the English teacher and photographer)

Nick Mulgrew is Zeus. Genna Gardini Apollo. Hoosen is the most vital organ of all. I think of the wildness

in their poetry, found poems, the education in the storehouse, the flame that burns inside Pettina Gappah.

Jewel of angels. Strange mental state. The curtain has fallen. The indigenous people have the sadness of the

beautiful. Your discrimination of me is unacceptable. Your discrimination of my delta of Venus, and all I want

to say is this. Bough down. My love of words comes from Alice, the love that I have for Jane Eyre. I accept all the

blessings that life offers. I silently bless everyone that I love, and who does not love me. I open my arms. To you.

Standing in the feast of the black whistling shade. I have become so pale. Introducing war, then peace, then there

are the gaps in my memory of heck. I am still a lover of tea. Of Malawi. The body of Judson Jerome. The renal

unit at the Livingstone. I accept Wislawa Symborska. Dancing chameleons you will survive me in a boat. A rough

boat made of stone floating through sea, river, and ocean.
At the wedding, I am a kitchen genie. At the parade, I am

a pale September. At the races, I am a blood spot incarnate.
I think of poetry. I think of peaches. I have to shave my legs.

I think of the ghost of day and night and what it meant
for child soldiers. Of peace and war, what do we mean by

anti-war. The anti-matter of anti-war. Night and the water
was vivacious. This is my voyage into eternity. Some have

hearts. Others have none. We are all pigs. Piggy snout.
Piggy lair. I live inside the music room. The ocean was my

first lover. It is a sea of green. Under the water I discover
Swaziland. I found a poem and it was fresh meat. And I

know sacrifices have to be made, that water never forgets,
that black and white are like fish fingers and chutney. Organs.

And so, I come again to my struggle with depression, my
winter has turned into summer's masterpiece. I regret you.

Older
(for my mother, father, and sister)

On illness, disability, and medicine.
I'm fragile poet, radical third wave
feminist, and my sister is happy, Slavic-
looking with her latest hairdo. She
is, and always will be, the centre of

my being. Ability to self-destruct,
lovely bones you have forsaken me.
Forsaken skull, frame, psychology,
framework of my skull, my celestial,
and nimble fingers, patella, nerve. You

centre of my being, every fibre of
my being, brain, this heart of mine,
platelet, aorta, and corpuscle. Why this
prophecy? My brother's smoker's chest.
Men in suits. All the time it is me. I

am a wonder made in the image of a
woman who is tough, who has guts, who
is not loved. Small enough for small
frail bird feet, do you feel old, I feel
old. It is inevitable that everyone is gong

to die. Burnt toast reminds me of the
English, and my aunt's fondness for
sardines, my affection for peanut
butter, jam sandwiches, dried fruit,

and apricots. There's a summer breeze.

At night, a draft of cold air through
the open bedroom windows. Winter
has its talons in me, caught me in its
grasp. I'm a different Dorothy Parker,
living vicariously throughout Ezra

Pound, Zelda Fitzgerald, Cole Porter.
Mute in a station once upon a time,
it was inevitable that this love affair
would have a tragic ending. Older.
I'm misanthrope. I'm somnambulist.

I walk alone now, with my angelic
tongue, instead of feeling intensely, I
don't feel calm at all. I'm poet-poet-
poet, film as art. I'm an artist in the
modern world, straining against illusion,

romanticism, love, love, love, the
older male, alive in the material world.
The lake is a ghost nation beneath
the stars, starlight, moon, moonlight.
In a station, he kisses me goodbye.

It feels as if I'm inhabiting a dream
world. I know I will never see him
again. This makes me sad, makes me
feel even more alive than I've ever
felt before. My thoughts are of lovers,

losing them one by one on repeat.
Mute, I'm a poet caged on an ash heap.
Regret nothing. Regret everything.
The women are wildflowers. Watch
their self-focus. The men plant, and seed,
and harvest their wives on a yearly-basis.

Jeremiah (experimental haiku)
(for my mother)

This ominous map –
Your skin reads like emptiness. (A giant swimming pool).
All-over taste Jericho.

Armchair shotgun shot –
You are green glass and amen.
Drops of blood slept here.

I have been harpooned. –
Butter up the bone parade.
Riot things of flesh-genie.

The bridge of language –
I wish my brother were dead.
I am moonsick ill-ghost.

Human rights mapped –
Jagged silence. Jagged moon.
Battered wife syndrome.

Lunch of blood. Mouthful –
In search of the mustard seed. (In the face of defeat).
The law says play fair-master.

A space to connect –
The trouble with violence.
You are not welcome.

These streets filled with dirt –
Think of the night-of-the iguana. (There's a library to keep me warm).
Smells of the cold. Teen-spirit.

Artists divided –
The time has come for now cosmic-Africa.
Main diplomacy.

Wife eating cold plums –
Major media in the-digital-divide. (Fugue on canvas).
Husband drinks whiskey.

Dandelions pop –
We struggle to write from any-point-of-view.
In plucking storage.

Fierce. Their prose is strong –
Hope. Young men and women all-powerful.
Unwavering flame-in-the-dust.

Pasted into the-body-snuffed –
Between man versus building. (Cathedrals dancing).
Cathartic posed. Self-less.

Macroclimate (experimental haiku)
(for my mother)

There is no one near –
I know much of loneliness. (The inheritance of loss).
I want to be loved.

You're you. A shell girl –
Flowers tangled in my hair. (I am a wrecking ball).
I want to be half-mad.

Is it too-much to-ask one –
I am christened Sexton, Plath. (I am tired of war).
This despair is a-tough-act.

I would follow you –
You said you-were-a homosexual. (I loved you anyway, thought I did.)
I called you state of-beloved.

Hemingway come back –
I relished the knowledge of-you. (As I would any lover).
You bid me goodbye.

You were lovely. Actor –
I never knew you. Not-even love. (Not even a love supreme).
No Rhodes for me.

No paths leading there –
Only to-Amherst community. (Amherst's halls and corridors and churches).

So, I write the mini-thesis.

Grateful for your love –
Little stars sabotaged me-in-the-end.
You did not choose me.

Doubting Thomas ill-advised –
Subtly jaded beyond the-stars-empires.
Where there is a lack-of-kin.

In-summer-rain I prayed for him –
He is noble. He is kind. He-is-a-mistake.
Child, your face is like-a-flower.

Pray for me. I'll pray-for-you-too –
The all-about-town men forget themselves.
Smoke. The sky is blacked out.

I am wrecking ball –
Know the inheritance of-loss-and-a-love-supreme.
I will forget you. (Never find you).

I purchased rivers (no telling why)–
(This) means leaving the past behind (for good).
Suffering crushing all-hopes.

Sappho
(for the woman I called my mother)

I mean to tell a legend. The voice
of resistance to love me. So, I write
to tell her. The he-woman in her to
tell her how much I love her, but
she does not heed the call, tells me
that she isn't, was never my mother.
It feels like a landmine, this autumn.
Suffering. Hunger. Miserable for a
mother's love. So, I give the flowers
instead to Socrates, worship Plato
and Homer. Praise Aristotle. I think
I know a gift when I see one. And
all I can think of is drowning in the
sea for an eternity. Subtly jaded as
the stars above in the heavens. You

were never mine. I stride regal. You
do not even think of me. Don't want
me around. I have heard you at night.
The sound of your knowledge was
like the rain of your tears. I have heard
the sound of your laughter. You have
walked away from me for the last time.
I think of the root's cut cause and effect.
You carried me in your womb for nine
months. Bipolar was then diagnosed.
You rejected me. Called me the black
sheep of the family. Dressed me up,

dressed me down as boy, boy, while all
I wanted was a lifeline to your heart.
I think of your starry womb. No children

have I ever had in mine. I am your
non-reality. I am your nomad across
the plains of the cosmic-Serengeti and
the Okavango. I compose you noble.
I compose you dripping from bathing.
I compose you America, just because
I feel like it. Go. You do not accept this
gift. It is time for me to leave. To give
up the ghost of you for good this time.
Sister is Berlin. Brother is dead to me.
Pretend I am the drug addict. That I
gave up my life in an overdose. That
I smoked weed, moved onto heavier
drugs while trying to find my way to you.
Morning you will find me alive. Gone.

No point in lying about the point of this
crime. This felony. This misdemeanour.
Take me. Take it all. Revenge is sweet.
You must love me. We are bloodline and
genetics. You say, but we're rivals, darling.
We're competition for the affections
of your father. You're the reason why
I can't sleep at night. Why the police come
to the house in the middle of the night.
I've sked you to love me, you say call me
by my name. Gerda, east, west. We all

love ice cream. I drink the soda that you buy. It is custom for the daughter to inherit the mother's earth, all of her material belongings, instead you give it to Berlin.

I would have died in your arms if I could. If you would have let me. There's no love left for me in this cold world. Everywhere I turn it is the centre of winter. I wish I was dead. You make me wish I wish I was dead; you see. I think of the nurses all in white bringing me back to health, while you weren't there to heal me. We sit together at a water table. There is no feast. Only jam and bread and fruit. I am trying to find you but you're a lizard. You're a Christmas beetle awaiting further instructions. I am mapping napping, trial, all the torment inside my head heaping up. You're a shard of a woman. Look at how you shattered me into a million pieces.

They're inwardly ashamed of me as if they could escape me. I am coated with shell-shock and combat fatigue. Angola. Still, still she won't love me. I turn in my sleep. I can't sleep. Counting sheep, then counting billy goats, then purring cats. Eating cereal at midnight. I need you to tell me that you love me, only for me. But you don't. Tired of your mental cruelty

after all these years, your rages and physical
abuse. I was good enough to be your
emotional punching bag then. Lights out.
You sleep like a log in a thunderstorm.
I am driftwood. The drowning visitor. You're
the morning star. Will always be my earth.

    Family don't want me around their
children. This time I am gone down the rabbit
hole again. I am mockingbird. Bipolar
she wrote. My territory and favour is
increased. The only one I love is gone.
I thought I would see the thief again, didn't.
Be kind to me, but no one ever is. No one.
If I was brave and free, I would be America.
Take down the veil from my intellect and
psyche. Let me eat white meringues for a
lifetime, and grow morbidly obese from
eating red meat, animal fat and eating. I want
something out of life, wonder what that
is. I want someone to tell me that I'm lovely,
but it is an impossible task. Mother, wake.

Smuts
(for my longsuffering mother)

You who never telephoned me once long
distance. The forecast was always rainfall.
Closure in the cement garden. Surefooted.
Thought I fell in love, but was just another
jaded romantic feeling. The hallmark of an
empty fantasy, father puts his slippers on.
The day begins. The day is over. Night falls.
I wish I could just disappear into thin air. Not
exist at all. I'm just holy smoke. A vision
in tangled wildflowers. Falling to my nape.
Wearing them in my hair. I smell like roses.
I smell like perfume. Wish I was born in another
cosmos. I have travelled, I flying across the
worlds of armchairs. I am harpoon-chaser.
Time and place and space. I want to forget.
Never the bridesmaid, never the bride. Find
me in the wilderness, in the fields of Hades,
let us harvest decay and Botticelli together.
I swallow bacon fat off my greasy fingers. Eat a
congealed egg with a spoon. The money is
in to pay all of our debts. The nurse, he had
green eyes. I thought I was in love, you see.
He had a girlfriend. He was in love, popular.
I thought I was in love, you see, in love.
Love. I was a beautiful child, once, once.
I am shot full of holes, crushing my fingers to
the bone, and I think about my father's

archives. Everyone is too busy in meeting all day long.
With eating food, with stroking the dog's ears,
I had such a healthy appetite for romance.
No longer rival. No longer socialite. You will
find me in a bed and breakfast pill popping
over-the-counter prescription medication.
You will find me there in the shallows breaking
code. I am a banker with the mad life of a
painter. Sister is Berlin, Bratislava, Slovenia.
I am not. Saw an enchanting bird, dreamed
up it feasted out of my hand. They call me
mad. Label me. Ate a hamburger to feel good
about myself. I am madness. I am madness.
Women kill me. Stab my soul to death. Call
me Aretha. I am doomed to this anti-depressant
nation filled with tranquilisers and psychiatrist.
I am hoping for meteorites this year and
flaming satellites entering the supersonic
stratosphere. They all laughed at me. All
laughed at me. Stoned me to death like a
martyr. Think of school prizes. How I long for
the corridors of high school. How I wish I
could go back there and start all over again.
Be loved, be accepted, be anything but older.
Be anything but nun, but spinster, but space,
just an empty space. Be anything but ruin.

Napoleon
(for my mother)

If my mother had loved me, I wouldn't
have grown up to be a writer. I think I
can still remember Napoleon's face if I
try hard enough. Maybe the dead will love
me for me, far more than the living.
Such a disappointment. No children of
her own, they say. She's not married yet.
The stink's been hanging around here for
days. I think of sorrow and the two wars.
I think of Krotoa. I think of Hankey. I
think of the streets of Johannesburg. The
birds of Johannesburg. The prostitutes
of Johannesburg. My mother never brought me
a change of fresh clothes in hospital.
No one came to visit me. No one called.
Telephoned. I have no house, no earth,
no world, no alignment to the universe.
I might as well have been dead. I think of
my learning like a cultural storeroom with
so much storage space. The lake is a stern
lake all winter long in Africa. I am left to
fend for myself. My lungs, my lungs are like
stems and roots and flowers. I am silent.
Have nothing to say like a farmer tending
his sheep. The bird is bound for the own
atmosphere. Light filters through the trees
in the woods. I am voyeur. The trees are like

voyeurs. I belong in this habitat for sure.
This thicket of thorn bushes scratching retina,
up my legs. My father wanted me to be
caged just like him. A madman, for a mad-
woman for a daughter. I am twin. Project Gemini.
I am a butcher. The image of the flesh
of red meat stays with me like a funeral stain.
I'm a shock. I'm a poem. I'm a negotiation.
I'm a parachute. I'm a pale September
dune. I'm a screen. I'm made of glass forever.
I am home. I am fur. I am atmosphere.
I put my shoes on, grab all the notes to
the orchestra playing in the background, make
off with you, Berlin sister, because you
intrigue me so, left me alone on my own
for years, neglected me so, and I wonder
will you still remember me at eighty years of
age. You will be surrounded by family and
friends. I'll still be on my own. You made
the break. You made the great escape.
You hatched the perfect exit plan, left me
behind to cope on my own. I am not like
you, not strong, or, brave like you. You
let me go like a weather balloon. Like science,
you let me go. You let me float away like
a lonely cloud, mapmaker, to the edge of conceit.

The Boer Wars
(for my mother)

Maybe I even look mentally ill now. Whatever a
mentally ill looks like, or, whatever bipolar looks
like, smells like, tastes like. I think of sly meanings,
hidden invitations swept under the carpet like that
one year we were invited to a family gathering but
never went. Uncles and aunts are like bookmarks, and
they don't want me around for an eternity's sake,
that's for sure. I eat twisters, and wings, and things.
To the edge of the world, to the edge of desire.

I try and let go of the roaring sea inside my head,
want to step into the waves, let the green seawater
cover my head for good this time, never coming
up for air again until I am good and drowned like war.
I think of the paths of my tribe collectively. If
only I was loved, not a problem child into self-
harm and the ludicrous, into droplets of blood of
the demonstrative-monstrous, and everybody else
knows what is good for me, except me. I miss the

hospital. I don't miss the hospital. Home takes
some getting used to all over again. I need your permission
to smile. I think everyone is my friend. I know
I'm not supposed to trust anyone for sure. I've
been like this for a long time. The world is outside of me.
This makes me sad, feel dejected. Feel less than
zero. I was very dark-skinned in school. Exotic-looking.

I am scared of everything. I am scared of everything. This human condition is still very much young.

Relapses come upon me. I bite into a green fig. I know, I know I can't ever live a normal life. I feel vulnerable and afraid. Don't want to think about the boy who has no name. One sock on. One sock off. Just got out of bed. Lightning strikes the air. If I could just be normal. If I could just stay sane, instead of slowly going insane all the time. If I could just get to university life, perhaps then I'll be safe. The sea is organic. Life cellular.

Oh, I felt normal when I was at the hospital. I was off my head mostly. Mostly in search of love, could not find it there, or, did find it there. Little runaway just wanted to be where the men were. Smoking cigarettes. I'd die if anybody read any of this. I fell in love, I fell in love. Felt orphaned when no one came to visit. Took the drugs that numbed the pain and made me feel dead inside like a wounded bird, or, carrion. The hellish tigers come during daylight.

The bear wife
(for my mother)

She is all-beautiful. She is all-calm. She is wise.
She is the full prize; wearing her crown for all seasons.
There's just room here for the inspired-romantic.
Nations dominated by the stars. Your descendants
will be fed. Follow the routes of the poet's journal
entries and you will discover a career in becoming
the bear wife. Early morning, give of yourself to
the world. Tidal, wonder, is what you are. I think
of your shared intimacy with your children, pose
after pose after pose. Your milk-fed voice is the winning
hush that comes to mind as does the toys of your grandson,
the books that he reads, your energies are sovereign,
you have taught me to remain in control of my feelings,
bear woman, bear wife in your wilderness your
garden grows like juniper berries, and dandelions.
I walked away from the hospital a green dragon

breathing flame, spitting fire, searching for self in ego,
excitement in monthly expenditure, I walked a
winter guest clothed in snow, chin defiant, the wolf
a philosopher who taught Nietzsche's language.
The bridge to getting there was cathedral-like in its
hectic-intensity shrouded in rare strategy. Anthems.
Nothing fades away completely without leaving
behind some knowledge that was lacking before.
The tree knows a rare intimacy with God. It stands
on the word, bear wife plan to achieve all your

goals today, this month, this year. Make your suppers known to the world by keeping the Sabbath as you keep the history of the Jewish people. To bless have the promise of eternal life prophecy itself must be manifest. Forgive us all of our sin, bear wife. I remember my struggles with depression with a

Peter. I was as fragile as a bird. Paradise was lost. I think of books, music and people. The comfort of strangers. I think of the aura of the sun, the spinning axis, the sundry planets yet undiscovered. This is not an ordinary world. Modigliani saw to that. This is not an ordinary life, bear wife. See, how your children walk after you? When the vision is written down; the vision is written down. Revival is the woman working for God. I think of translation and breakthrough, think of eating, think of the faces of love, all-scholars of trivia. Kiss the boy who lives in the house with the tin roof. Kiss the rose in the cheek of the girl whose heart is as cold as the centre of winter, worship and adore your daughters. Think of my madness, and the madness of other people. Dance stanzas.

Lull
(for my sister)

A grief observed in the shadowlands. Parachutes
in September. I want you here with me, but you're
not. You're spending Christmas in Berlin sister. You
don't understand the choices I've made. I don't
understand yours. I think of the alignment of bipolar
in spring, I think of the voices in Africa, the gifted
focus of wildflowers in bloom. Everywhere I go
I think of you in Berlin. I live in the shadow of the
rhino. You meet people all the time. Make friends
so easily. I am purpose and all-plan for the year
ahead. Trying not to feel the tired-happy pain of
losing you to another sun, another moon, other stars,
another country. Bratislava. Slovenia. Budapest. It
is good to see you have a European-future inside you,

of you. That you have a special love in your life. I
miss you so, so much. Think of you daily as if you
were still living in Johannesburg, a research strategist.
I had Europe as an idea in my blood. You followed
her through. Went to Pretoria. Left me far behind.
Church seems to help. Adoring God with others, you
seem to be in the same room with me, damselfly-on-
the-wall. I think of your tangled hair in your hands.
Your Moroccan oil on your hands rubbing it into your
hair. It is just mum and dad and me, and your brother
now. The characteristics of childhood are over now, you're
gone. I think of the yolk of your manners, think of you
standing there with shock, with terror as if I could

bring you back somehow to me. You could live again.

There is a monster under the bed giving me a fright. You're amazing. You're my half-truth that turns the key inside. I believe in diaries. You believe in packing a suitcase, traveling from country to country across Europe. I believe in futurists escaping their pasts. I still cry myself to sleep thinking of us, thinking of you in another land, on another continent. I think of the sunlight falling on your hair, the trick of the light in your eyes. Once I believed in you, but that was before I knew how to fly. How to focus on the fact that I had wings. Anti-matter at my disposal. The voices, I have never stopped writing to you, my Hemingway, Rilke inside my head sound very far away now. I have had a good rest, if I can call peace that. I still don't like the dark.

All roads lead to Grahamstown, come back
(for my mother)

Saturday you are leaving for Germany, sister.
At night I sometimes dream of Africa's hunger.
Reality is rarely revealed by the winter rain. The
light war is blinding here. I look for you as a
girl child in photographs. Your smile so fierce
and sudden. I long for you to belong to me again.
Your heart is my heart. Your hands are mine.
Angelic source of pain, you're my wound, you're
part of my soul, the surface is on fire, the lake
is frozen solid, the swimming pool where I was
baptised, where we swam every day after school
as children is open to the public. It is going to be
a long summer. You're not here. I expect you

to show up all the time until the sea breaks loose,
and I dream of going to Rhodes like our father
did. My sadness makes contact with the wilderness.
My jewel in the dust, are you sunburned in winter,
when are you coming home, I feel as if I am
trapped here waiting for you. Open the trapdoor,
let me out. This is both apology and love letter.
You are invited like a courier. Stared at like a
pageant queen. I've asked you repeatedly to love
me, this diary of an insomniac. Childhood continued.
So, you rose above your circumstances. I failed.
You're still playful and sweet. All of my roads, my paths
lead to Grahamstown. Come back. Come back,

my love. Where is your home? Who is your
home, my love? In the early hours of the morning
I am working on my novel. It is about an alcoholic.
A hiss, and I melt like ice in the glass. Eat bredie, install
the African Renaissance in everything that I
write about. I want you to feel the cold like I do.
I feel dead inside without you here, without
you near. You're making a new life for yourself.
You're making a new world for yourself that
does not include me, or, us. It functions with you
as the sun. This is preparation. Feels like it is.
For a long goodbye, for a kiss goodnight, for
a never-ending story about nostalgic starry you.

You are clay applied to my womb. Your eyes
don't seem to see winter in Johannesburg
anymore. You are a tale of two cities. One lost,
the other found only in memory. I think of
Godly people, who we worship, your tribe of
friends. Your German boyfriend. Thank you for everything.
Thank you for your help. Thank you for making
every year especially memorable. My first love,
how are you keeping without me by your side (as
if you ever needed me)? I have loved you my
entire life with the lightness of my being, then
think about what I write. I write to celebrate you.
The world seems to say, make something of it.

Sultanas
(for my mother)

I think of the mind and times of the wolf,
the corridors of high school that I hid in away
from the world, I long for the worlds of
the storytellers, a culture-stricken society in
which I am actor and songwriter and director.
Cool people don't think that I'm that cool,
that I have just finished the touching up of
the palace of my great novel. I think I have
always been three women in one. Architect-
designer, inventor-scribbler intertwined with
daughter-sister-vulnerable orphan. I see a door,
three doors, three women short story writers,
a dysfunctional omen, the superego of an ex-
boyfriend who was the masterpiece of my life so
far, my so-called life. He never touched, or,
kissed my soul. I am so tired of loving these
ways, this blow is strange and almost primitive,
and I am tired of loving. The sea enters me
so, in a roaring succession, in possessive ways, so,
I dance the hours away, silence touching the
Amherst of my community. I search the nightfall
for the moonlight that marks the way of the ones.
The thousands of stars until dawn breaks the
intelligent crowds of this city going home to
their land, their country, their nation, and this
lull. I have become like a ghost. I live like one too.
I am perfectly cool and wise, all I want to do
is look inside, move mountains, all the stars are

here with their cosmic auras, and I think of the wise blood within me, Galilee, rivers and lakes filled with fire-breathing boys. I'm in a cave, then a dune, and I become a leaf. Shadow on the coldness of the wall, autumn leaves are as fragile as my heart, we all begin as clay animals, something uplifts, empowers them into life. Life goes on, life carries on, love dies, love triumphs, and I think of the ocean, the perfect ocean, as we are, as we are, off the stage I leap into the page, the empty page, sway my arms like branches because here I am beautiful and perfect and wise, you will never look within me, too scared at what you will find there, too scared to love me, all of me, all of me. I think of you, Berlin-sister, standing on the rooftop of a building taking photographs of the sunset. You're in the arms of Germany now for two weeks. You're not thinking of me. I'm thinking of you so perfect. Say you love me again and again and again and hold me close like you'll never let me go, go, go. I think of the silence found in all of these hours. The grass is greener, the pastures are explosive, you feel the cold because it is snowing where you are, you'll never know the fears I have for you.

She sleeps alone
(for my mother)

It is the day of my nephew's wedding today. Dagga joint
in the bathroom as usual. Nobody looks at me when
I-want-to-crawl-into-your-bed. Took a long hot bath.
The alcoholic chokes on the white meringue. Burning
in the rain. It came from Japan. Empty skies. Portrait.
Miracles in-the-house-with-the-ghost. Childhood. Self
leaving her sorrows behind. Heart of gold should be
river dust, dogs barking wild into the fall of night, an
olive-skinned woman with a sensitive face, not-so-young
woman carries a purse and her mouth is pale and quiet.
A man carries a blank slate where his head should be.
I ride a crazy horse into Jerusalem. The season freezes winter
over. Winter has drugged the leaves, what the body was
made for. Mine is pharmaceuticals. There's too much dark
forest. You're a lifetime ago. Something hurts. Wounds
me to the destruction of old people. I am a surgeon's glove
in the science of winter. You are so random. So, so basic.
Sometimes I can't stop looking at you looking at her. At her.
Walls we built. Nothing at all. You're gone. Oldest, oldest ex-
friend, you're the silent scream inside my suburban-town
doll-heart. I swim in a swimming pool, begin again says
the emperor, anything is better than being alone. I'm frightened
to
death of being alone. Having no one around when I am older.
When I am elderly. I eat toast with orange juice. If I was
yours, I would be pure again. Everything hurts now that
you're not here. Every time I look at a picture of you now

I start to cry. I am a modern woman. In my dreams you're
not here. When I wake up, you're still not here. I'm tattoo
on the bound. The way things are you're in Berlin, or,
Prague. Life has changed so much ever since I was a Indian ghost
girl. I sometimes want my old life back, when you're
were around. I am ballerina. You are poet and short
story writer. You are world traveller. Not home for the holidays,
Christmas again this year. Yes, it is called desire. I still
read your star signs. Don't use my broken heart. You
don't call me. You speak to mum. I think of you speaking
in broken Czech. You're gone. Never to return. I fell
in love with a room that had a view. All I am thinking
of is starting a war, the music separates us from thinking
of happiness and its pursuit. I think of taking you in
the dead of night away from here. But I was far away from
here, from this Eden, this sprawl, from this swamp life,
from this path of adventure. It does not matter anymore
that you don't love me, me, embryo any more like you
used to. We're chameleons, that's life, souls are what we are.
You're young and perfect. You're beautiful, incubus, and
you know all the answers to this world, and this ochre
hanging earth. I miss you, everything about you, everything.
I think of you walking the cold streets of Berlin, of, constellations of
Rilke's Prague. I think I am starting to let you go. Husk of angel
wheat.
All that time, I would love to waste it again, with you. I think we
suffer as Einstein suffered, as Mozart, as Prince, as Elvis.
You're clouding up my mind. Taking sides. Wishing on a leaf.

The Unstable Genius of Jean Rhys

I can hear his voice in my veins. He calls me his, 'Porcelain-darling'. Sometimes in my flat here in London I would move from one room to the next astonished at this 'love-experiment' I was delving into. I was now once again 'a work in progress' as I had been as a child in Dominica. The first man I ever loved made me feel more of an exile on these London streets. Far away from home, the only home I had ever known. It was the known. Love is like plasma, floating mitochondria, atomic particles, the accurate building up of ignorance into life experience, the harsh, neon underground bricks of illness. Love for me was always an unlikely dilemma. Do I or don't I? Sometimes I think we live with ghosts. Love is a ghost. It is ancient as illness but it makes me bleed at the starting line. Curtains at the open window of the hotel room are moving in sync with my little bleeding scarlet heart. Why do I write? I want to find myself in eternity when I'm in heaven. Everything has returned to normal. I am on my own again. I don't want to strike it rich or land me a guy to marry me (both at the same time would be a dream). There will be no reunions with family, with lovers, with 'him', that kind, sincere wealthy man I first met when I was such an ingénue. He taught me the difference between the words, 'authentic', 'squalor', 'but these are terrible living conditions', and 'you can even find human nature in a symphony if you listen close enough'. He taught me the meaning of words like, 'the brittle movements and accurate moments of solitude', 'how to be astonished at how ignorant people were, how vain women and men were', 'all pictures always carried powerful observations of life in the details'. I would hear his voice everywhere I went in the beginning stages of our relationship (I called our little affair). His voice healed some parts of me especially when the dark air of night was advancing. 'God is mostly in your head but most people do what their hearts tell them to do.' 'Life is boring and we need activities like love to get us through the day. We're a match. People think life owes them something if they're not born rich but even rich people are lonely and ignorant. They can go to the best schools in the world, but are they educated, no, cultured, no. Have you ever felt abandoned, neglected, ill at the thought of being rejected (I felt like that my whole childhood) I wanted to ask but was too afraid to, too afraid he would think I was a mouse, weak. There was clarity in that. You need to think more of yourself, Jean love. You need to express yourself. If you feel indignant, feel indignant. If you feel confident, feel confident. Don't be so afraid of the world around. What is the worst thing that could happen (I already knew, that someone could laugh in my face, stare me down until I looked away but I never confided this in him because there was no reason to)? Sometimes I think you feel terribly lost. I see a terror in your eyes as we leave one another. You remind me of a lotus flower and for me it is the most beautiful flower in the world. He could articulate it (love), show it, examples of it (I could only describe it, make plans for it for the most part in my head, connecting threads of the purest thoughts of it in black notebooks). I was his pretty doll whom he spoke of in whispers to in the dark. Jean, sometimes I think you are hiding something away from me. I think an entire wonderland must exist inside your head for your own pleasure. What sweetness that must come with. It must taste refreshing. It must taste like pink happiness, a deposit of charm in a room that has not felt it for days, for my Jean, my bird without wings. And so, his champagne voice would carry me through the day and for most of the night for this insomniac. Sometimes I could feel the stress on my heart, its thudding, hammering away pressure and there was nothing in the world I could do about it. All I had to do was to live. I would watch children sometimes and think to myself what their gifts to the world would be when they grew up. Sometimes my heart would turn to paste as I watched them and I would think that now, finally everything had been taken away from me. I could never be free and then I would walk down back streets. There would always be an undeniable lightness in the road's blackness as evening began to settle all around me. Its magic fingers in my hair, the wind rearranging my hat, massaging thoughts of rope and poison, putting stones into the pockets of my coat and walking into a lake filled with ice and trees at the bottom into my mind's eye. I would think of the dilemma that faced Romeo and Juliet and how sometimes when I was feeling very low how that same dilemma faced me. I wanted to be myself but not on my own like this. I knew I had failed. I did not know how to get back to life. I did not know how to dance to modern society's beat. I did not know what modern meant anyway but I knew I was a most modern woman attached to absolutely nobody and nothing. And then the tears would come streaming down my face. I could not stop them and why I. Life would had not been fair to me. I did not know anything about modern acrobatics and the flying trapeze artist was a comic to me and sometimes my mind's eye was a width of a thread and it was simply connected to nothing. Some days I would feel brave as I if I had a destination in my step but I knew that was a lie. Soon everywhere I went I would hear his voice in my head, as if he was with me in the room. 'You can survive anything, Jean as long as you put your heart and mind to it. You look beautiful tonight, simply divine, and come here let me hold you. It feels as if it's been forever since I've last seen you.' By that time, he was already a ghost. It didn't feel real to me. His voice had no substance but it kept me company, the illusion was so strong. I didn't know how to distance myself away from that habitat of his beautiful house filled with fireplaces, flowers and pictures hanging on the walls of landscapes, a wine cellar. I just wanted to dissolve. Sometimes you live poverty. I've lived in poverty. And at first, I didn't want people to see me like that. You know, drab, pathetic, old clothes, out of fashion. Funny, but it made a difference to them, made their hearts and their diplomatic hearts and heads softer towards me. They exhibited empathy to what I always thought was my unlikely demise. They gave me money and I would use it to live as best I could. There was an understanding. Out of sight, out of mind. It was fine if I was going out of my mine with loneliness so long as it was on their terms. And when a guy (I really don't really his name, how we met), he finally he broke off the affair a few months later he was very diplomatic and suave about it. Although I couldn't understand how he could be so composed about the whole deal. To them money meant success. I had no money. I wished sometimes that I could distance myself away from it, my love for it but I needed to live like other people did, don't you see. Whatever that word 'normal' meant it gave me Goosebumps just thinking about it. And then in the end I thought it was normal to distance myself from society. From London to Paris, Europe what a pilgrimage, what a privilege. Whoever gets the chance to travel these days? And then I was soon back in London again. Whatever happened in Paris had been an adventure but now it was over. Sometimes I felt vertigo as I was walking on those London streets. I felt blessed with the knowledge that somehow, I was perhaps writing for a generation that would come years after me in a golden age. It was a generation who was now experiencing life as children while I was a grown woman. Sometimes I thought to myself I was not meant for this world. In the evenings London would become a ghost nation but I did not want to be stuck in a room. It was too depressing. I became too aware of my current situation. It would make me feel sad. I would feel like having a drink and then my whole outlook on life would change after I had the drink within me. The man who lived below me would knock a broom into his ceiling and ask me to 'keep it down in there' (whatever the hell that meant). I didn't know what on earth I got up to in the early hours of the morning. Sometimes I thought I would just be writing, scribbling away, staring at the walls. I would think about love, how much I really liked the idea of it. There are a lot of things in this world that are rotten, unpleasant things to deal with. In the evening or usually when I am alone something always seems to loose-itself violently from me. Sadness, a wounded feeling as if I almost don't belong in this world and in a way, I know I don't fit. Perhaps I am too reckless in the choices that I make. Perhaps I am not a safe person to be around. Too much of a thinker, brooder, reader always keeping love and the attraction of it in the dark until I can feel pin points of lights trying to break through the cracks. I am no good. I am bad at love. I am bad at affairs and matters of the heart and bad at relationships. I must rest now. Tomorrow is another day. So, I wait until the room is filled with darkness and I listen to the noises in the street outside, downstairs, in my own room. And I know I've walked that street today like a ghost as if I was not aware of my surroundings. Soup is always good for the soul, as are confessions. Here is one for one. I don't believe in the death of things anymore. I believe in life as much as that is hard to believe. If only someone knew me well. If only I had a companion. If only I didn't have to suffer for my art. All of my life I watched women in their relationships with men. How they would smile, turn their head, their eyes watchful and waiting, how they would smooth their hair down, arrange the food, the salad on the plate or cast their eyes over a menu and how the men were pensive, eager to please in this sunny environment. How could I have known then as a child that I was not one of them? And that I was never going to grow up and be one of them? I would watch these women always smiling; listening (but were they really listening). And I wondered why these women with their fine clothes, elaborate hats, and brooches why never spoke back. They were always nodding their heads like puppets. I knew from an early age I was not too pretty so I would have to work hard, but also I would have to discipline myself not to be too smart. I reckoned that people's lives are meant to be celebrated when they're alive not dead. There was always something pure about the day as I set about my walk and there is something to be celebrated in that. The union of life mixed with the elixir of what I drank (and I always thought of it as an elixir). I was not built like that, to be tough I mean. I was never meant to be a bully or a tyrant. I just did not have that warmth in my voice, that kind of spirit flowing in my blood. If poetry is an elixir then prose is food for thought. I've walked past people and they've stared at me. I've looked away but sometimes when I really think of getting to grips with the situation, I want them to try and understand me so I stare back. What do they see, a casualty disconnected from the rest of the world? I live so simply. My life is easy and cheap. My supper is usually bread and cheese. It is always bread and cheese. No change there and my hands smell like soap and this room's bare bones creak under my stockinged feet at night. Writing has become my ritual. It has become my escape from grief and raw anguish and frustration.

Sometimes the process of writing torments me but I also feel very anchored by it. It's therapeutic, it minimises the stress that I feel thudding inside my head and it gives me a sense of purpose. All the words seduce me, gets under my skin. It is so intense, this pleasure that unravels and seems to release the chill out of me on cold nights. But I can no longer feel the weight of the world resting on my shoulders so acutely. The words seem to paint that blue pearl into a rainbow of magic colour. Into childlike stuff of fairies, dust, a water wonderland, into soul and life, everything of beauty and not a disturbing sense of things. I always wished as a child to make contact with things like that, magical things. I'm thirsty so I get up for some water. I can still taste the salt in the air coming in from the sea in Dominica. Why would I go back? Sometimes I remember why and sometimes I don't. Fast forward to a flat in London and I go by the name now of Jean Rhys. A name I have changed so many times. I have no money, no skills, and no form of employment. The cheques come regularly. He called me a 'porcelain darling', 'daring good girl', 'special' and that I was 'loveliness personified'. He had kind eyes. He was so authentic and a real gentleman. I mean authentic in the terms of he was a man who was made of substance and everything around him, his home, his household, his wealth felt real to me as I entered the foyer and stared at the flowers in the vase that seemed to welcome even me. I believed nothing was wrong and even when the affair ended I still thought perhaps there would be contact again and even a friendship but years have passed (the poet in me I guess came up with these foolish notions). Realising that the past is past even the temporary frightened me to death. But there had to have been some reward, something golden that I could get out of the equation of knowing this man and coming into his world even for a short period of time. I could not solely have duped myself into thinking, into believing that it was just a lark on his part. You know that whole easy situation. I could think about these things for hours on end, fill my entire day on the he said she said transmission of our conversations. Sometimes I would get stuck on a sentence, just the tone, how he would express himself and it would drive me crazy, up the wall and I would will my brain to dissolve it. It would feel brutal but brutality in the end also serves its own purpose. It will make you realise that you need to rest. I don't know quite when I've finished with something. When I have to quit it but I do know when I have to rest. When I'm kaput. I'm too young to know about those sorts of things, that's what I wanted to say at the time. I was thinking it all the time watching the creases in the corners of his mouth. How the fleshy part of the skin in the middle of his forehead was crinkling up as he watched my reaction. I know he was just testing me to see if I would fly out of control, would she make a scene? How would the past few months come to an end? I felt like an orphan. I shouldn't say things like that but that is what I felt like. Lost, terribly afraid of the world, neglected, abandoned, no home, no name and family. There was no hope in damned hell to resurrect my lone self. There were parts of me that were wolfish, that was the part of me that could fight, battle (I have the scars to prove it) if I had to. No, if I was challenged. But I also withdrew easily and that was the weakest part of me. It didn't matter what kind of climate I found myself sheltered by. I embraced skating on illness and when I did, I yearned the most for my art and all my little rituals. Now I am tired of the years of cold I have lived through and this incessant hunger that I feel for attention and most of all my neediness. Violets were my favourite flowers in the world. Maybe because they're so pretty and cheerful they make me feel that way. They don't make me feel like death, volcano dust or blue warmed up. Sometimes I dream of my mother's fingers knitting, not braiding my hair. In the middle of the night I come upon a sleeping world, a dream world. I journey there for a while pacing back and forth, sometimes crying, sometimes in a sombre mood before I fall asleep myself. The stars are like birds in my eyes on the nights you can see stars in London. They are like birds with their wings outstretched. Ready to meet the oncoming edge of the sky or a sword of air. All 'Ella' had was imagination and she kept that close to her. 'Ella' was always secretive and I have kept that because if I didn't I would have come undone a long time ago. I am what I am because I have wanted people to believe it, especially other women. In life there are always choices, pleasure, desires. I always kept waiting for love to change everything. A Prince charming and as dark as an Arabian knight in shining armour to rescue me. But life never goes according to plan although I am an open door. Sometimes it feels as if I come alive in the dark. The sun is like a mirror. If it's there I never see it. I am not conscious of its light, and my reflection in it. I can feel (I've always been aware of this for what feels like forever) the dark side of life more intensely than the lighter side of life of it. My hair was not spun gold. It was dark. I did not believe in fairies and their wings or that Dominica was an island but I did like the trees. They were my favourite and the open fields and when a spell of tiredness came upon me, when I couldn't breathe because of the heat I would imagine. My goal became to fall in love with warriors in suits who had wonder guts in their blood. I've loved many and I've lost some along the way. Splendid confidantes that I held in high esteem as if royalty. I've learned to go on loving although it is the hard way. You go on paying the price one too many times. There's a flaw in passion, a conspiracy in love, that hate that always cornered me on the playing fields of childhood that seemed to flow my way as a gauche chorus girl. You know once upon a time there was a man who wanted to adopt me. I think he wanted to take care of me and be a fatherly figure. Some kind of mentor, a friendly man who would keep me out of the firing line of the inquiring gazes of others who would exchange company for money. One last time I am more in love with being in love than anything else. The air is crisp (a tattoo on the green landscape). It feels as if I am living in an ancient world collapsing under meteors. What does progress mean to a writer? Write more books but they have to have a market and they have to sell well but the writer must always be morose and depressed. Very difficult when it comes to giving interviews. I do not know what impact my books have on the rest of the world and I would like it to stay that way. I know that human behaviour is predictable. It is also a precious cargo. But I am made of glass. Why call off the splendid search (such an adventure) for the adventurous spirit at heart, that instinct. I am the feminine lark, the songbird. In my line of work there is such a thing as clarity but no such things as clocks. What is the meaning of that four-letter word l-o-v-e? And when it is nailed to my heart why do I stammer when I speak, why does my heart beat to another rhythm, cadence (I can hear it as if it has gone underground somewhere). I have to mine it like a mineral deposit. In love when I have fallen, fallen hard all my thoughts are hushed up, meshed together mystically. It is hard for me to understand men sometimes, to have a concept of them as an object, to understand their failure to communicate and the world they inhabit, their domain. The sense of their beliefs and mine differs profoundly. They can be monsters made of winter, coldly inspiring all kinds of aches and pains of the mental kind, cerebral but they can also incredibly vulnerable. I ask myself, do I want to write. I can't remember when I wanted or started to write. When I received that inclination from the universe. I only knew that I had to write to save myself. I don't remember when I remedied the thought of not dreaming with drinking. Alcoholism and crazy seemed inseparable and here is when the writing comes in, rescues me. The writing was always a useful exercise. I never learned to smile those early years in London, never believed I was a rose among the thorns. Perhaps all young women are supposed to think like that (that is what drives them, for the better part of my adult life it haunted me) and feel insecure in the bloom of their first love affair. I was not a flower, could not wrap my words around the tones of crisp English. But I remember the tears. As a child the back of my throat is a land of thirst. I knew that there was something else out there for me. Something besides the loneliness, the sadness and despair that I sometimes fell into, that became my child's mind-sanctuary. Dampness seeps into the lining of my coat. There are flecks of cloud in the blue sky. But is it enough to want desire? The faded grass under the leaves under my shoes. The faded grass under autumn leaves, Whitman's leaves of grass and the sacred contract that existed between human nature and nature. The woman in the park she will not appear the same in a photograph as she will in memory. This Eve taken from Adam's rib who was a daughter doing what her mother did. Woman, the ethereal girl figure turning on a pedestal with her eye on the prize of love. I have my observations of them, these others, glorified futuristic poster girls for motherhood (who would in a few years' time settle down for life). They will live as they dream in their sleep and dream to live. And all my life I have wondered what do children communicate when they laugh? Turkish slippers small enough for small frail bird feet, a gift from a friend. A draft of sunlight in the air burns bright. I am held, caught up in its grasp. Illness has touched the glinting, sharp parts of me. It is not the bag of bones why have you forsaken me, my skull, my frame, celestial nimble fingers, and patella. You centre of my being, nerve, every fibre of my being, brain, heart of mine, platelet, aorta, and corpuscle. Why this unfinished prophecy? And then it grew cold. It is as if cosmic force was holding all those clouds up together. The world around me, its people, and the rich became wealthier, girls on the chorus line retired from the theatre life when they got married and everything around me moved forward. It got its talons in me and I never became that selfless kind of person I wanted to be. Darkness falls. At my core lies gravity. All my life I have wanted to be beautiful. I have everything else. I will never get married. It is all becoming a bit too much for me. A bit of losing my mind, my heavy head giving way. I can't keep lying. Keeping on and on with it. I must be honest. I must be truthful. The unopened bottle of gin is there on the table. I must stop wasting my time. I must be brave and throw my head back and love, laugh in the face of adversity. I must stop wasting time. If I don't eat something I will disappear, that superimposed elusive part of me, the soul, the frightened part, and the physical and private body of the subconscious. I am becoming a non-entity. I can become used to the idea that I do not exist in the material world where the others meet. Men and woman of similar interests and backgrounds and who have common goals, that connects them to each other. The morning air in my room is cold, heavy and still. So I make way to the kitchen to smoke and although there are rats in the ceiling it is not all doom and gloom. The writing life has chosen me. Being happy is a unique state of mind. I can remember when I felt as if I was let loose on the world off the ship from Dominica to go to school in England. If only I knew then what I know now. London wasn't a distant place, it was a distant planet. The results can be electric when opposites attract. I could dance but I was not good enough, not graceful, less than the other girls. I could act a little but then there was my West Indian accent. So, in the end it was decided that I was a terrible actress. I could not cry on command in class instead I started to laugh and to laugh and to laugh and that drew attention to myself. An artist works with materials at hand. Voice, the life force of the body, touch, hand movement, eye coordination, physical body, and the senses. What can be more precious than to be coloured by an auspicious space and when the abundant universe gives you wings? To start from (childhood) and to transition it from a dream (to act on the stage) to a comfort zone (ending up in the chorus). Sharp, blistering, in a brutal dissolve came the comments when I was younger living in a house with other siblings, a father for a doctor and a mother who was always certain that I would fail if I set my heart on anything. Threads, connected by them govern us as we are by the books we read. I have a theory about books. In the long run they will make you wiser but they will also make you cry, laugh, as wise as an owl. Deep unhappiness can be challenging, that and learning to fight your battles. What many people don't realise is that egocentrism can be good for you up to a certain extent. Especially when you are given a stage, an expectant audience (a waiting one). When you are expected to shine brilliantly. It is egocentrism that wants, drives you and that gives you the ability to do well (ambition), expect a rousing applause, admiration, adoration, a standing ovation and to a certain extent love and acceptance and your abilities for being recognised for what they are. Why is simply achieving happiness so hard? The negative ruins optimism. It ruins me for good. When I was younger, just a slip of a girl I wondered what having a backbone meant. My first prince did not love me. The most that he could give of himself was never quite enough. I wonder if the vegetarian restaurant that I frequented when I lived in London is still open. I ate the noodles and the soup it floated in heartily while watching the world go by. In those early years I was afraid of what was going to happen to me. Would I ever make it? Would the lady in me ever come out, deserving of love, out of the hole, the void? This scared cat. I'm frightened of people who constantly tell you that they love you. Truth and beauty exists in a microcosm of things. Scientists will say it is atoms while I say I am a voyager and these are the sum of my parts. I believe in having interests and sticking to them. Having goals sometimes gives me light-headed feeling. Is that what I am really supposed to be here for? It makes me feel locked up, as if I have to have a witness or witnesses for everything that I do and envisage for my life. I am always struck by how unsure I was by the cruel wonders, how filled with dangers the world was once. I did not become immune to it quickly. Do I have my upbringing to thank for that, I do not know. I feel lost sometimes when I stare at my reflection put out by unwanted visitors who go from door-to-door but I also feel pure of heart too. Men have done me no wrong, that charade is long gone. It is I who have been foolish and reckless with my own heart. You see why blame them. I miss the sea and the view from the top of the hill in Dominica. The horses we had when I was growing up and when I got on that boat with my aunt that day to say goodbye to the world I grew up with forever I asked myself, what would I do in the world? Would I always be petrified, would warmth or the cold always strike me? I was always the curator of wish-fulfilment, dreams, an odd sort of museum where nothing fit because there was no culture to, and no sanctuary. There were moments in childhood when I despaired not having anyone to talk to. I remember the sadness that seemed to pale everything else in comparison. I wanted to be happy but I didn't know why I wasn't a happy child. Why I never smiled like the other girls? I must have been too quiet. I must have been a mute. I must have been a dark mute with a dark soul, intense and always burning rough around the edges. No, I was never like the others. Not like my sisters with their lovely faces. I am not perfect. The perfect partner, co-conspirator, somebody's wife, the perfect daughter, and sister. In the end it is just a not too long list of words. I never wanted to be alone. I did not want to navigate the world flying solo with fingertips caressing maps. I will never forget Paris. I will never forget that I lost a child there and had a daughter. I am a mother, a writer and perhaps I wasn't a very good wife. Of course I went back to Dominica but it wasn't the same. I was older and London had changed me for good. And perhaps it was the snow. I could never get never get used to the cold you know. The fires that always had to burn (what a waste of fuel) and I never really took care of myself in London the way I did after I got married for the first time, second and third. After the third one I had money from the writing part of my life. Past is past but it was on a certain level it was never quite for me. I distilled it with my pen. Childhood wounded me. It still seeped into me somehow. Through my clothes and it got to the very heart of lonely me. At one point I must have looked like a bird, as thin as one. London wounded me, as did relationships, insights into the observations of other lonely people around me (I would watch them through the window at that vegetarian restaurant or sitting around me at the other tables). Tiredness that crept into my voice. And then later my spirit. I was always ready to fly off the handle. If not now, when then. When will the world begin to become fascinating to my bright eyes, my bright intellect? When will I become fierce? I was an extra in the movies once but in the end it did not count for anything. It did not turn into anything. I was still the same old same boring me. And I cried. I would write into the night and I would cry when the rest of the world was sleeping and dreaming or coming out of a club into the empty London streets. And in the morning when I woke up with the rest of the world I felt complete in a way I cannot fully come to grips with or make you understand. And now after all this time that has passed me by, I feel ethereal. I have faced the angelic. It has taken me on and I have won. I am otherworldly by design. A design not of my own making. It has taken years. There is always a lesson in love even though you may think for now it is wounding your spirit. I was a bride. There I said it. There was never a word for this pent–up sadness that sometimes felt poetic. I just knew I was on edge for some reason. I could never be the mistress of this bright and new force within me. Freedom like any consciousness- thinking awareness is a psychological construct. It is nothing more than that and if we think it is going to be more, we are going to be sadly mistaken in the end or we will realise it too late. I was once a daughter then an orphan. I had the maternal instinct in my genes. It had to have been there. To know that kind of love and be on the receiving end of it anchored me. When I held my daughter in my arms I had never felt more at peace with myself. My daughter's childhood songs, her many sweet, curious, inventive faces, the avalanche of presents I bestowed upon her on birthdays and Christmases. She had a father and that was also in a way a gift from me to her in a way even though the three of us couldn't be together, live together properly as a family. She was beautifully well brought up. When do routes become important? I fear only in later life. When you are too set in your ways. When my dear, you are old and think you are going crazy. What would it have been like to watch the Dominican sun setting in a sea lock-and-struggle? I would have given anything to see that tonight. When you're in your bed at night with the thick covers pulled up around you and think you can hear something in the kitchen (when it is only a window you left open or a cupboard door that refuses even with the wind to bang shut). When you think that someone in the dark is out to get you, the bogeyman. I've journeyed. I've journeyed and have no regrets. The living keep on living while the dead turn to dust. Nothing really belongs to us. When we leave this world we take with us the possessions we arrived with – the lone self. Beyond evening's contours are the stars and even further out there is the moon. And if I close my eyes, I can imagine being aware of nature in or touching the sky. I already said I was a bride. But I cannot remember if I felt passion that day. Of course, a ring did mean that now the two of us were now bonded together for life and that was with my first marriage. I had a passion for libraries that mildew smell, the ancient pages that almost seemed to wilt in your hand; those lose pages that seemed to have come undone. I had a passion for books, above all for notebooks I could scribble in to my heart's content, and I always loved to read. How do you shine if you are not guided by 'other hands' and by those 'elders' who had come before you in the world? Pain of the mind can be more devastating, felt more acutely than pain of the body. In my life there was always the baby, the sister, another sibling has taken my place and now overshadowed me in everything I did. How do you know you're alive? You find poetry, the way of the writer with all the cleansing rituals in the space of the writer, the table, the chair and water to drink, bread and cheese for a meal. And slowly I slip into a routine. I get up in the morning. I smoke. I brush my dishevelled hair. I go for a long walk in the streets of London. I am not yet that famous writer who is now elderly, famous-enough to have a driver to take me around town and pick up parcels before he drops me off at home at a small cottage in Devonshire. And after my walk I must write. I confess. I had a cat once. It was a proper Persian kitten but the people who looked after it didn't look after it really well. The poor thing died of neglect. And then I was sad again for a long time. You have to have a heart to get yourself attached to animals. This is my voice, made of gossamer, tasting like the season's fruits or cauldron (take your pick). It is a voice that sounds like Keats, and I am offering it to the world. It is I who have closed doors on myself, escaped through the window that was left ajar and not the other way around. And these are the notes from a writer's journal, my notes. Shut the door. Shut out the quiet light. Tell yourself to swim away from the tigers with arms pillars of smoke. One day I will find myself in a forest without men, without huntsmen and warriors, nomads and ghosts that burn all hours of the day and night. One day I will dazzle and fizz like a champagne virgin (hiss like a cobra). I will laugh in all their faces. I will weave and thread stories, braid hair and dwell in possibility. My mother taught me that. White Knight you jewel. The bluish sky falls off you. I prefer the word 'solitude' to 'loneliness'. White Knight you jewel of Hollywood. One day I will shut the door. One day I will shut out the quiet light. One day I will tell myself to swim away from the tigers. My tingling arms pillars of smoke. What a pale and beautiful creature you are (you once were upon a time now worlds apart) but are you happy? You went on to paradise and wrote and wrote and wrote and won prizes and planted flags. My beautiful creature as cold as all things that come from the sea, the lover of love and picture of health. I have bits and pieces in memory of you of other peoples' keepsake stuff. The mouth so angelic and so grateful to be kissed and the eyes like dew. I knew at the end of it you would still have a soul to come home to. Alas the same could not be said of me, dude in black, cowboy in black. To yearn for love, to live in that paradise again and again and again is a wish granted to a chosen few, the chosen ones and what happens to the others? The others live to exist for their families, raising their children or for themselves, for their ego. If there is no love to feed you, nurture you, caress your tired or grief-stricken face at the end of the day then I imagine that there are people out there who sometimes feel as lost as I do. What can loneliness communicate to you? It is a lovely feeling. You're freer in a way than other people are. But who is there for you to talk to at the end of the day? People need companions. People need friends and family, loved ones and acquaintances. People need contact, closure, and relationships. There are people who build empires on these kinds of things. And then there are people who need, want, desire love as wide as river, as deep and beautiful as the Pacific. And then there are people who turn their back on that and embrace a life guided by the pulse that tells them to be brave. And to turn their back on a world that calls them an Outsider, a loner, strange with strange ways of doing things, a strange way of thinking. And you just have to have the courage of your convictions if you are this sort of person. I am this sort of person. So weirdly out of sync with the rhythm of other women my age. So good am I am at this thing, this sly-odd movement that I have won prizes for it. It feels like a bird's wing in spasm in the air. It feels like a rush of warm, sweet air into the beautiful red ribbons of your heart, a cry in the dark, a promise that you make to meet up with someone in heaven at a deathbed. Someone dear and truly loved who has passed on from this world into the hereafter. What's eternity anyway? A more novel, adventurous dimension because it becomes lovely when you think of it in that way. Not meeting up with strangers but meeting up with familiar faces. The faces that you knew, loved and cherished since birth. They were people who were always a part of your world in one way or another. So I say one day we'll all meet in heaven. We'll make our way there from all of our other destinations that we 'lost' a little self, worth and identity in. Everybody is married in some way to his or her soul and every bit of our soul is intended for and to be hitched, hooked, stitched to God. Whether you want to believe that or not is entirely up to you but to me it makes sense. I love the useful wonder in thinking that. And then there are those lukewarm questions that tug at the puppet strings of the heart. Not floating suspended by nothing but an existential breeze in the air, not drowning just there, behaving mysteriously as if they had all the right in the universe to be there. When I was in love I wanted to know everything about him and nothing at the same time. Falling in love, head over heels, sweeping flaws under the carpet did not come with instructions. I did not know how to correct something I did wrong. Everything was new and pretty. To love someone since you were a child is a very long time. Illusions, they do not come with flaws and they cannot love. They're too much in love with themselves. People do not ask, 'What were you like in the womb?' Men do not say with a great amount of insight, 'You seem to have been a fish with the spirit of a lioness even then.' They're answers for the volcano dreamer. The last battle was always touch and the solution for me is this. My sister and I had a conversation and it went something like this. We ended up not really saying anything at all like most of our conversations these days. God can keep your soul. Let me bury you there in paradise. In no particular place in paradise. In your claustrophobic world where you were so cold. You white knight death cutie on parade. It's the little deaths in pixels from childhood that is as nutritious and forgetful as dreaming. These days everything is crisper. Images are sharper and brighter. (And now what about the men). Of course the men are in secret code so they can never be discovered out. In a mirror I see a wife (always a fretful wife with screaming, crying babies). 'Poor babies,' I enjoyed saying and why didn't he love his beautiful wife more and why was I the chosen one. I couldn't really see why inexperience was so sexy. There is nothing barren about this man's ego. But his hands always felt cold. He had dark, dark hands; skin like velvet and even his eyes were dark. They were always so full of concern for me. I pretended it was wonder. Living your life and moving forward is the easy part. It is the forgetting that is the hardest. I can put a face to a name, city, and occupation. I remember. It is all in the details. I don't want to meet these men in heaven or in any place else. The men with all that sadness, rage and perfect-wonder in their eyes. All their faces look the same to me and after all this time I did not step back from the picture and say I forgive this and I forget that. They look at me as if to say, 'You too had a role in this. A part to play in all that drama.' The drama felt quite useless to me on the one hand and like jazz on the other. 'You're quite mad, you know.' One man told me but he couldn't exactly look me in the eye. So I bravely posed in mask after mask after mask. Another man preferred 'the girl'. Well, that was his thing. He didn't want educated, intelligent or smart. He didn't want cute. He wanted 'the girl'. He wanted a pure, angelic face in beautiful clothes. He wanted obedience. He wanted to be put on a pedestal and worshipped. And so, I did all that. I couldn't quite understand why because I could make conversation but he never wanted to talk and understand how claustrophobic I felt sometimes just being in his presence. It felt completely otherworldly to me. These things called love or rather, 'the affair'. It didn't exactly feel like romance to me. No, there was nothing romantic about it. I feel a great deal of shame because I did not listen to my heart. A heart that was telling me his wife meant a great deal more to him than I did and even on a certain primeval level his wife's body meant a great deal more to him. She had given him children. And he had built the house they all lived in (the one, big, happy and boisterous family). But since this is my secret diary it is just between you and me and nobody else has to know especially my father. I don't want him to think differently about me and the life I chose give or take a few years ago because I am not that person anymore. And I don't believe that time heals. When people say that it is as if there's something specific to time. There's nothing specific about time and even clarity doesn't even figure into it. I can ask my ancestors why I've never been lucky in love. Why I've failed so dismally in that department (much too much of a daddy's girl)? I can say I will never give my heart away again but I don't believe that. I usually fall in love up to three times a day. I was just starting to feel hungry. And when I am hungry I have my breakfast, usually toast with a smidgen of butter (from a brick that's been standing out on the kitchen table or counter since the following night) or margarine. And I make myself some tea. Just toast (brown bread toasted in the oven like in the old days and I smile when I think to myself that I am from the old days now). I wake up earlier and earlier and go to bed later and later. It feels good to be thirty-two. I didn't feel it (old, stale, as if I was coming into a rut, the state of the nation, the world my generation found themselves in) when it was my birthday but now that the next one is around the corner I am feeling it. It feels like too much effort this morning to make an egg, boiled, fried, or scrambled into bits. So, I'll have my toast with jam this morning. I think of him and everyday it doesn't hurt less, it hurts more. I've given up on humanity. What I see on the news or the little I read in the newspapers terrifies me. It scares me half to death. Children raping children (aren't they just babies), the desolation of poverty and how it isolates people from the mainstream of society. What is relevant to me in society is not relevant to the media. They write what sells and it is usually salacious material. Here today, gone tomorrow or the next week until it comes back as an update or haunts you when you least expect it. It is funny how the mind can play tricks on you especially when you're over thirty, reaching that point of middle age. The news often pins down the status of refugees, painting the women with their children, food aid flown in from abroad, white tent after white tent in a field of white tents and again there are stories of rape and mutilation. It never seems to end. We are capable of many, many things. God can keep you soul and man will take and take everything else. I never thought of myself as a fierce person as a child. I was an introvert. I never thought of my mother as a bully although she could be quite fierce. When I was in London I hid all my diaries at the bottom of my suitcase and forgot about them. In London I would meet a man. We would eat noodles at a restaurant or go out for a drink. In Paris life was different. When I would meet a man there we would go out for a drink at a café. The lifestyle in Paris was like that. Drinking sparkling wine into the early hours of the morning. I would become a different person. I liked myself more. When I was with a man I told myself this was it. This is what passion felt like when I was in his arms. This was love, beauty and when it ended, when we went our separate ways there were days when I felt I was going out of my mind. The loneliness, the fear that I would never have that again made me turn to writing. I would open up the black scribbler. I would sit and think to myself isn't that the most perfect word in the universe. In the middle of the night in my stockinged feet I would just glance out of my window and watch the world go by, trembling, chilled to the bone, drinking milk from a chipped mug. And I would write and write and write. It would simply pour out of me like rain from the sky while I would sit in my room. And so a book would turn into the pages of books, a stream of thought would lead to a threshold. I could now connect threads from my past to my present. I could still remember the ice house of my childhood, aunts, visitors to the house, voices, a mother who did not have the heart, the slightest idea, nor inclination to love me. She could murder chickens though. Strangle them by their necks. In a way she strangled me too. Perhaps when life is hard for women when they are girls who always have to compete for the love of their father that kind of intent is simply woven into their consciousness. Stars. Stars. I never see them in London but the night sky in Paris is full of them. I wonder how I will look in middle age when beauty and appeal and the sex drive, that impulse when a man is drawn to woman will fade. Life is poetry, my childhood in Dominica and women with their ammunition and their apparel. I never thought of other women as being in competition with me for the approval of men until the end of my first love affair. And then there was the poetry in my twenties. It cut me deep from skin to bone. I could feel it you know. There was nothing dysfunctional about the cut. Only I felt its power keenly, its voice, the chains and links of the voids therein. It stated wish fulfilment, commentary on modern issues and I felt it intensely at night when the world around me was asleep, when I felt drowsy or secretly despair at the situations and conflict I found myself in. Sometimes I even hated myself because I knew with some finality now that I had created the world I lived in now. There was no going back. Childhood, whatever state of mind, flux I had created then and now was over in a strong and futile sense. I could never get it back (whatever normal was). Normal was a word everyone used. It was a word everyone around me, even my family believed in. It was a word that depressed me. Was I a lady? I who was so ignorant of many things, that had so few belongings, not even a tiny flat or house with two bedrooms to my name, furniture that I could move and place in rooms as I pleased. Had I ever really been in love and loved? I believed that secrets should never be told. But I told my first husband everything. I wanted to believe that he loved me completely, that the past didn't matter. Back and forth I would go every night writing effortlessly in my black notebook. The past, history came with such ease. In this day and age the woman I had become was called a non-conformist. The norm was to get married before you were thirty and have children, a house, housekeeper, maids, a linen cupboard, have holidays, go camping, to the seaside. Of course I thought I would and could have all these things. I would have worked for it but shock and horror it did not come my way. I was left behind while others stronger than I was took that shot at the big time. I shook it, writing all my secrets down (the parts of me that just did not fit in this life, this city). I shook if off my chest like a fish hooked on a fisherman's line shook the breeze and seawater off its scales, and fins and back. Sometimes I thought to myself, 'Jean, you're missing out. You're missing out on life.' Sometimes I would say to myself, 'What if you'd just let yourself go a little? Talk a little, make a little conversation, be brave, braver, and confident like those mannequins in the window that you passed today with their chins up.' I thought I would only become illuminated as a woman when he, the man in my life stroked my cheek, my palm, my bottom lip, my head and it would always come with a rush of this feeling to my head. He is so pale and beautiful, so fragile and delicate, like a flower in the winter light. The hush of silence in the room is as soft as feathers. His breath is as fresh as water. His soul is perfect but he doesn't know this yet. I imagine it's a feeling he will only experience with his children and his future wife. Now he is a work in progress, caught between two worlds and enjoying the view. It is as pure as white-hot chemistry. His eyes are wet and dreamy. His hands and his fingertips are not delicate. They bruise the wasteland of my face easily. When I was away from him the world around me became cold. It felt like a feast of winter all around me. A heavy glow, inviting look, a picture of innocence colours your look of the world, of how to be loved. Tonight, I am an empress of cool in my dress and for a time now there has been no new money for new dresses. It hurts so much when he touches me on my arm, when he puts his arm around my shoulder I shudder. I can sometimes feel the chill wrapped in his embrace. His fingertips burn my skin, my lips. The only thing that soothes me is his kisses, his presence and the fact that now in the bedroom we are equal. Now submission, role-play, pain and pleasure are open to interpretation. He is gentle around me tonight, he is not angry, emotional or abusive, hurling abuse, screaming at me. His day must have gone reasonably well. This relationship doesn't heal anything in my past; bring emotional closure to the abuse I suffered in my childhood. It only serves to encase my newfound promiscuous behaviour in Technicolor in a bubble, in a grandiose time warp. I can't make him love me. Yet he is just as much impossible to love with his own mood swings as I am. I am always forgiving of his artistic temperament. I ask myself what is his heart, his soul trying to express. He's just as wounded as me. Comfort me, hold me just a while longer but he doesn't make eye contact with me, and speak to me. After making love I am as empty as a drum. I watch him sleep and feel fiercely protective over him. No love lost, only my innocence. Before I was invincible, and now in his arms I am fragile and delicate. From far away I hear myself say, 'Say something funny. Make me laugh.' He smiles, looks at me as if to say, 'I am not in love with you' but I don't care. For now, he is all mine. He belongs to me. His body, his jokes, the smell of his aftershave, his stories, his eyes, his lips so soft and delicate and bruising all at once. He is bitter. He is sweet. He does not believe in me, he does not believe me when I say that I love him. In my heart I say, I'll take you just the way you are, you maladjusted, maladroit, abusive, abused child from one abused, damaged and neglected child to another. He can see me and that is enough for me. I wash his back in circles, making ripples in the water with the palm of my hand, talking in circles but he doesn't say anything-meaningful back. I know he's just using me, humiliating me and causing a future exposure to trauma. I don't know any better, anything else, any other life. What is the reward, what is the payoff? Even when he humiliates me, he is still looking at me, working miracles on me. I have become an addict. It doesn't matter whether or not he speaks to me with contempt. I am convinced I have nothing without him. I am convinced I am nothing without him. Look at me, rescue me, save me; but the lost boys with vacant eyes and vague promises never do. They leave me feeling haunted and blue with ice water running through my veins. They never smile at you until you smile on the outside. If I am quiet it's because of the urgency in his voice, his breathing, his movements (himhimhim). Shame was a word I heard often when I was a weak child with a raving mother who often taunted me. And in this ice house there was no beauty, prettiness, loveliness, only grief, weariness, and a cry in the dark. I could not be alone and feel that kind of fire. And at that time in my life and in all the faces I saw around me all I saw and heard was, 'I do not, I do not, I do not love you.' And so order was spoiled and chaos ensued. I became frantic and believed that Lolita's passage had set my own. I kept my heart in a jar and my head in the sand. Everything happened so fast that I had no control over the pressure, the tightness of the close-knit and newly formed friendships, the disturbance, and the disturbances. I felt I could no longer live in a world that was not accepting of me. So I had to create a character in a storybook, a fairy tale to be loved, a glutton for punishment. For me he would bruise me to the bone, to my psyche. I'm a dazzling insomniac. Even my silent screaming when I am falling apart is dazzling with my every waking thought and living moment. I brought submission to the table. I had solitude on my side. He had a kind of self-leadership about him then. I was alive even in those empty moments. I learnt to say, if you feel like it then love me, if you don't then don't. I began to see his, my, our rituals as crucial turning points in the relationship. I could not bear being alone, being left alone. The headline read, 'Let's stop the persecution'. It could have been something I had written, perhaps a letter to the editor. I saw a flash, a slap against a face across the breakfast table and my sister gave a shout and began to cry. I remember washing my hair in a woman's salon and reading about the virgin lover in

Nabokov's Lolita. My fingers holding onto the spine of the book, bookmarking the last page I read. The girl sitting next to me at the basin had doll eyes. They were brown with gold, golden flecks in them and so I began to learn what any woman would do for vanity in high school. As a child I grew up in a house made of brightness, made up of bright things. Tough love was a shiny bullet flying through the air. The surfaces were conservative, tense yet tidal, emotions running high, the collection of them and those experiences hard. And then I began to long for the weight of the meditative hush in leaves. It was the only thing that brought me peace of mind and that froze both joy and deception in their tracks. I wanted to be the sensible child taking the separation or divorce pretty well. I wanted to tell my mother that she hurt the people who loved her the most. But he, my father does not give of himself effortlessly or consistently. There were often closed doors. They would bang shut and it could be heard in all the rooms. It could even reach children who were supposed to be asleep, their ears. It couldn't have been that serious. I heard my mother laughing. She sounded free. Free in the sense that she was a young girl again without any limitations being placed on her. The limitations of a family and a husband and especially work. My mother and sister had the personality of a volcano. All I could taste was rain, pretend that I was dead in the sea whenever, wherever I heard a shriek of excitement on the beach from other children building castles. I imagined auras while their mothers dried their hair with a towel and gave them money, pressed silver coins in their hand for ice cream or for something cold to drink. Other children would parade and dance in front of their mother's. I wanted to be left alone. I was always a child on the verge of a nervous breakdown. As a young woman I wanted my gracious, appreciative heart to locate others. The art was not to fall like the virgin lover in Nabokov's Lolita. But fall I did. It was always cold where I was. It was not my dream to be endeavoured with literary pursuits from a young age. Children do not have the mental faculty to wish fear away in an instant. Children are just brave. They just seem to have that cosmic life force. I don't think I was a brave child. I wanted to be a volcano but I just didn't have that in me. And when I grew up into a young woman, into a writer, that oppressive feeling that I had to be emancipated in some or all the way never left me. It stayed with me at my side. It was my doppelganger. And as I became a vibrant type of person and my thoughts more and more vivid I could see all the beauty in the world around me except in me. All I could understand was people and write about them and me observing them. Playing dead in the water in the end had served me well and had taken me to new heights and had fostered an unseen intelligence. My father did everything but talk. Meanwhile I pulled out the entire minimum stops and shortcuts. Purpose is life. The war inside my mind is often a war of nerves, a crowded house. It leaves me with a feeling of being locked up inside a box, Pandora's Box. There's place for stigma and being, the unbearable in there as well. Living in a fog-like consciousness, always watching the clock, that round island made up of numbers. So I had to discover that the universe promises the human condition two things: mortality and eternity. Depression doesn't come with a vision of the world. It comes with its own canvas, blank and its own personal mission, do or die, go beyond yonder. The proof of depression is something absurdly supernatural, that there is something greater than you are even if it is a calling and a gift in your blood. Your need to learn how to fly, the machinations of your consciousness 'caught by the river' by the river exploding into life in front of your eyes. Sometimes the story begins at the end or with flashbacks with dramatic effect moving forwards and backwards. It is blood that is thicker than water, than family bloodlines or the phoenix rising from ashes. Head against the brick and stone of depression is often a permanent protest. When I began to write poetry, I left space for interpretation, for kindred spirits and soul mates, even for ghosts. It is brutal, dissolves, deranges, distorts and it drums this in to you. It has such a presence, pain, depression, melancholia standing at attention. Poetry became my goal (the force of my reality, the reality I lived in) and my life. It became my desire that existed in both the spirit of place of darkness and light. It became the psychosomatic root to my cognitive thinking and my self-help. When you're depressed you keep your thoughts and reflections to yourself. They're more often than not charged with electricity, electricity that is not easy to shield yourself from like the eye of the sun. 'Come back to bed.' Your body says. Your eyes are vacant hinting at the spark and the glow of the displeasure of ill health, old wounds and escape. You feel naked, as if you've been abandoned in the dark, the pitch black and thrown to the wolves. I make lists of things that trouble me when I feel depressed. Any female writer would write what she feels destination anywhere in an upside-down world. Nothing fades away except the material world and the physical body. And so then I found myself in the city of cities, bereft, sinking my teeth into the polished floors of the library, the archives, the newspapers, textbooks, novels and biographies, anything that I could get my hands on and read. I was a film student marching across asphalt and green armed with books and not so often an engaging intellect. If only people were more like me, I wondered. If only people were not so mediocre. If only the other students did not spend their time drinking so much, not understanding me, sharing cigarettes. And then there was the woman with a feather in her hair, a modern-day witch. Her skin dark and ashy she would dance mad with rhythm in the halls of the ward in the hospital with feathers in her hair. I could not understand her, the mechanism, that shift within her brain, whatever was in her head, that swift shift in the chains of her consciousness like leaves against grass, Whitman's Leaves of Grass, Lewis Hyde's The Gift. It was here that I discovered Goethe. All I could think to myself was that this was madness and that madness could be as magnificent as the highs of euphoria. Nothing unique but as weeks went by it didn't seem to fade away into the comfort blanket world of inhibitory drugs and prescribed medication and that beautiful Lithium. I could only face the world with the psychology I gleaned from my reading, delving deep into the ghostly facets and facts of the unstable planet of illness and mental illness. I grew excited by the potential that lay ahead of me, in the distant future. It was always hours away. All I had to do was built on the edges of a dream. When I think of that time before my life began once more in search of a fabulous road, I seemed to live in a nation in ruins in that hospital, filled with ruined people, and lives that were intensely fragile. Their sadness seeped into me like stains in the peeling wallpaper at the Salvation Army. I needed to feel alive and I could only feel alive when I was witnessing the pain of other souls and when I could tell and see how the world put pressure on them to excel. I began to live in books and on the plateaus and landscapes it offered me. I needed to picture a life without the cool order and routine of student nurses hovering, staring at a television's snow. For now I needed that but I needed the world too. Dark, dark, dark and just like that it was gone. I am the way I am because of my mother, other women, my father, aunts and the hidden meaning in responsibility. I have felt devastation all my life, loss, people simply passing through my life going from one place to the next and I have found that words are the easy part. The outside world doesn't inform anything that you say or do when you are living with ghosts that you're waiting to be cured of. His eyes were a sea of green glass and his hair was long and dark. We could talk for hours sitting on the grass. I would stare into his eyes and that glass would chip away at the fragments of my heart. I even found time to fall in love and out of hate with my soul (what is does it mean to have a soul) and with the being of myself. I found I could reconstruct the material, make it emotive, and make it glad. I wanted to bring my family back together again. I wanted to heal what was broken. All I saw around me were broken people, shattered people, people in recovery under daily observation and I was one of them. I felt as if there was some part of me that didn't belong to the world. Yonder, unbearable light, madness, illness, scar tissue, a heavy kind of woundedness can do that to you. And what are women truly at heart if the writers are the thinkers. Poets are dreamers and being conscious of their dreams they are conscious of the guts they have to live in this damned-if-they-do, damned-if-they-don't-world. We have to start somewhere I reckon, all women do. We are the ones who have to come up with a blank emotionally intuitive and spiritual slate before our written words become imprinted on an audience, a reader, a woman, a man or a child. Before we burn away into nothingness, before we escape, and before truth stares us down in the face. Awareness and the grit in our souls always comes with nurturing and until there's an unbearable lightness in our awareness, a turn of the switch to develop this spirit in others. Our writing (female writing) only becomes more successful when we inspire others to gravitate towards greatness. From a youth's pure and angelic roots to being a walking mass of contradictions as they grow, to their bones, the consciousness of a movement has begun across the female nation reaching converging lines bordering on the universal. Writers' psyches cannot survive in dysfunction without the pictures of our external reality growing cold and dim as they fill inner space, marking turning points in time, in the flesh of history books. This is my message to the youth of the world. Pay attention to your dreams. The light in all of you is like a volcano. It can melt the heart of stone. Perhaps one of the loneliest experiences in the whole world is this, writing. I say this because on the surface I feel I can make it look effortless (there is a transference, a catalyst that I can't explain, can't put my finger on) while inside the vision we have this surface that if looks could kill it could kill. I've realised through my long walks that the woman who is secure in her home is the woman who has married, who has those children, who cooks those breakfasts and steaks, maintains a household, is the lady of the house. She is the madam who orders the kind of fish her husband likes to have. She puts honey and lemon in her tea, serves it like that when guests come to her house. Other women her age, other women with the same interests she has, who have the same number of children that she has. She does not have to put her coat on, her scarf, and her hat and open the door and walk out into the world a leper, yes, I say a leper because she is rejected wherever she goes. She is the Outsider, the loner, isolated. Nowhere is there a paradise for her. There are norms and values. What are the norms and values of a single woman (note I did not say the single 'lady')? A single woman is a burden to her family if she is unemployed. If she does not have any skills and her loveliness fades away swiftly. Nobody wants to have anything to do with her. They do not want to talk to her, converse with her because she does not have any talents. If she had they've already convinced themselves of this fact that she would've been married long ago, off their hands. She will never find herself in a field of love. Instead she will imagine what it would be like. She would imagine the atomic illusion of it. And she will know deep in her heart that she will be a girl for the rest of her life, a being who will never be swept off her feet by a masculine swagger. She would never understand what the words 'flirt', 'flirting' meant. She would remain detached from the world her cousins now inhabit, tangled in obsession. Men like to eat meat and she will remember meals she had with a man once or twice. How he licked the fat off his lips and drank his wine and how kind he was to her like her father was and when she thought of that she would always think of Dominica. You have to live. But I didn't know. I didn't know how to live, how to ask, 'Are you happy now?' All I seemed to say over and over again was, 'Are you happy now, Jean? Is this what you wanted, or was it a manifesto of loneliness and despair that I had been searching for all of my life since childhood?' All I knew was hotel room after hotel room, meetings there, situations there. I wanted to be filled bit by bit with love and empathy for other people who seemed to find themselves in the same situation I was in. They were lost. I was lost. I was scared to find out that I had no substance. I was baffled by the life around me and the lives people were living. It was as if they were telling me I was the fraud, the fake, and the poser. I still don't know how it came about, the writing part of me that bit. Now when I come to my younger sister she is half otherworldly, half superimposed in reality. Now she is made of substance. God, why am I not. Why? So here I am? Why? I don't know what love is, what love is made of, why I am out of touch with that reality and I've been out of touch with it for a long time.

So here I am in London where the lights aren't as bright as they are in Paris and in my dreams I was in Dominica. It was always playing at the back of my mind. There was nothing European about me although I had travelled on the continent. A man gave me advice once. I didn't take it. Oh, I pretend to listen and it's alright for them to know that I am just pretending too while they pretend to care about me. What are you thinking about in that intelligent little head of yours Jean? I don't think you need saving. I think you're fierce enough to understand your circumstances, to grapple with the future that lies ahead of you, to take it on. Not many women can do that. Are you lonely? Even I get lonely sometimes. Sometimes even when I'm surrounded by other people truly living. What does it mean to truly live? Does it mean to be happy, and content, the weight of a ravaged country or mountain off your back? Money does not make anyone happy. It can make you, give you a certain sense of power and control over other people but coming back to you, pet; you give me that impression that all 'little Jean' had known in a way her whole life was suffering. It is a reality I can't bear to face, to face this existence, this depression, this illness. You might think I'm brave but I don't think I'm brave. There is nothing heroic about miserable me I'm afraid. I sought out male companions who were pure of heart and failed miserably at that too. While leaves curled up (I too curled up in my bed at night), shrivelled up (my soul shrivelled up), winter danced away and seasons passed, turned into the loving of summertime I took to the streets again and little cafes. I casually observed the ballad of the human race around me and the wonder of loneliness. It took guts to live and I was so meek, so week, mousy. I did not know how to live. Nobody had taught me anything about that. I had to steal it the best way I knew how. By using my brain as a catalyst and by filling black notebooks with the winters, the breath of the wilderness, the wild of life, the Technicolor of poppies in a field, drops of rain on a drab coat, shoes that looked a bit worse for wear. I wanted to remember Dominica (my choice). Not the suffering but the lavishness of the books I stuck my nose in the library when I was a child. It made me feel better. I too had a right to live in this world. You, anyone could not take that away from me. I was not a ghost although I moved like one through the streets. I have finally decided what my gift was to this world. Sacrifice. I am still here. Magnificently I am still all here. The unbearable light in having bright conversation, sharp, bright, intuitive eyes with insight into the world around sensitive me. I need a drink, badly, to forget all about yesterday. I'm pensive (don't give a damn about this maddening hell that seems to cavort beautifully, helplessly around me. I drown in its echo, its phenomena.) Am I cultured? Am I educated? I always wanted to be. I wanted to be a woman who is secure in her own home. I wanted to be a brutal thinker, a woman who has not been initiated into the sexual impulse (the wonder of a kiss, the virgin seed awakening to consciousness in a touch, love, beating heart, romantic interlude) at an early stage of her development. Poor me, hey. I don't think my mother ever knew how much she really hurt me. I think when I first became aware of that I became less trusting of the world around me. I became detached from it in a sense and there I was thrust into a state of imbalance. I could no longer feel the flux of equilibrium, fisherman's thievery, the glint of the silver skin of the fin of the fish. Love stories come from that place, the land of immortals. They truly last forever but love affairs are another equation, another seam, hemmed in by mirth, priorities and cons. They're inelegant. A love affair drifts. You can't read its palm. It has a noose tied around its neck. It lost itself into the world like it has been there forever. It's just an obsession. It is just an obsession in an open love field. I met someone once. He smelled like the earth. His hands were rough. He wore a mask and I had one too but it didn't matter. It didn't matter that we couldn't define the boundaries of the relationship. He made me feel as if I could do anything, be anything, feel alive. It was as if I had just come into being, you know. And when it rained, I didn't feel the rain. When I was away from him the world no longer felt uninviting and cold, grave and condescending. I could look people in the eye because now I too was a possession. The dark no longer made a cripple out of me. It no longer burned me, that giant. I could close my eyes and fast forward to a time that I looked forward to. I no longer said, 'What is love anyway? It means nothing to me.' I would sit across from him at a table at a restaurant (he would order and he'd be in charge) and he would say things that would fill me with delight, with bliss, something would just shift inside of me. I would no longer be a girl; I would become a woman, a fashionable lady. I would sample everything on my plate. I would warm to him. The days when I felt persecuted by sitting idle while the world would go by would be long gone. He would colour my life now. He would lecture me not my subconscious, and not the inner spaces of my mind. I'd think to myself that now I have no more adversaries. Now I have my revenge. I only have to compete with other women who are in my position. My lonely days were over (not completely.) There was a part of me that knew that there would be a new area where desolation would await me. I would be hungry for more shades of energy, power, and love. As soon as the person or people in the next room or downstairs moved out, someone new would move in.

Mmap New African Poets Series

If you have enjoyed *Nobody Loves Me*, consider these other fine books in the Mmap New African Poets Series from *Mwanaka Media and Publishing:*

I Threw a Star in a Wine Glass by Fethi Sassi
Best New African Poets 2017 Anthology by Tendai R Mwanaka and Daniel Da Purificacao
Logbook Written by a Drifter by Tendai Rinos Mwanaka
Mad Bob Republic: Bloodlines, Bile and a Crying Child by Tendai Rinos Mwanaka
Zimbolicious Poetry Vol 1 by Tendai R Mwanaka and Edward Dzonze
Zimbolicious Poetry Vol 2 by Tendai R Mwanaka and Edward Dzonze
Zimbolicious: An Anthology of Zimbabwean Literature and Arts, Vol 3 by Tendai Mwanaka
Under The Steel Yoke by Jabulani Mzinyathi
Fly in a Beehive by Thato Tshukudu
Bounding for Light by Richard Mbuthia
Sentiments by Jackson Matimba
Best New African Poets 2018 Anthology by Tendai R Mwanaka and Nsah Mala
Words That Matter by Gerry Sikazwe
The Ungendered by Delia Watterson
Ghetto Symphony by Mandla Mavolwane
Sky for a Foreign Bird by Fethi Sassi
A Portrait of Defiance by Tendai Rinos Mwanaka

Zimbolicious: An Anthology of Zimbabwean Literature and Arts, Vol 4 by Tendai Mwanaka and Jabulani Mzinyathi
When Escape Becomes the only Lover by Tendai R Mwanaka
ويَسهَرُ اللَّيلُ عَلَى شَفَتي...وَالغَمَام by Fethi Sassi
A Letter to the President by Mbizo Chirasha
This is not a poem by Richard Inya
Pressed flowers by John Eppel
Righteous Indignation by Jabulani Mzinyathi:
Blooming Cactus by Mikateko Mbambo
Rhythm of Life by Olivia Ngozi Osouha
Travellers Gather Dust and Lust by Gabriel Awuah Mainoo
Chitungwiza Mushamukuru: An Anthology from Zimbabwe's Biggest Ghetto Town by Tendai Rinos Mwanaka
Zimbolicious: An Anthology of Zimbabwean Literature and Arts, Vol 5 by Tendai Mwanaka
Because Sadness is Beautiful? by Tanaka Chidora
Of Fresh Bloom and Smoke by Abigail George
Shades of Black by Edward Dzonze
Best New African Poets 2020 Anthology by Tendai Rinos Mwanaka, Lorna Telma Zita and Balddine Moussa
This Body is an Empty Vessel by Beaton Galafa
Between Places by Tendai Rinos Mwanaka
Best New African Poets 2021 Anthology by Tendai Rinos Mwanaka, Lorna Telma Zita and Balddine Moussa
Zimbolicious: An Anthology of Zimbabwean Literature and Arts, Vol 6 by Tendai Mwanaka and Chenjerai Mhondera
A Matter of Inclusion by Chad Norman
Keeping the Sun Secret by Mariel Awendit
سِجلٌ مَكتُوبٌ لِثَائِه □ by Tendai Rinos Mwanaka
Ghetto Blues by Tendai Rinos Mwanaka

Zimbolicious: An Anthology of Zimbabwean Literature and Arts, Vol 7 by Tendai Rinos Mwanaka and Tanaka Chidora
Best New African Poets 2022 Anthology by Tendai Rinos Mwanaka and Helder Simbad
Dark Lines of History by Sithembele Isaac Xhegwana
a sky is falling by Nica Cornell
Death of a Statue by Samuel Chuma
Along the way by Jabulani Mzinyathi
Strides of Hope by Tawanda Chigavazira
Young Galaxies by Abigail George
Coming of Age by Gift Sakirai
Mother's Kitchen and Other Places by Antreka. M. Tladi
Best New African Poets 2023 Anthology by Tendai Rinos Mwanaka, Helder Simbad and Gerald Mpesse
Zimbolicious Anthology Vol 8 by Tendai Rinos Mwanaka and Mathew T Chikono
Broken Maps by Riak Marial Riak
Formless by Raïs Neza Boneza
Of poets, gods, ghosts. Irritants and storytellers by Tendai Rinos Mwanaka
Ethiopian Aliens by Clersidia Nzorozwa
In The Inferno by Jabulani Mzinyathi
Who Told You To Be God by Mariel Awendit

www.ingramcontent.com/pod-product-compliance
Lightning Source LLC
Chambersburg PA
CBHW070847160426
43192CB00012B/2344